THE YAVAPAI

The People of the Red Rocks
The People of the Sun

by
Kate Ruland-Thorne

THORNE
ENTERPRISES

Sedona, Arizona

by Kate Ruland-Thorne

Editor: **Aliza Caillou**
Cover Design: **Ron Henry**
Printed by: **Sedona Color Graphics**

ISBN: 09628329-5-2 paperback
Library of Congress Catalog Number 93060648
Copyright 1993 Thorne Enterprises Publications, Inc.
Second Printing 1994
Third Printing 1995
Fourth Printing 2001

ACKNOWLEDGMENTS

My very deepest gratitude goes to David Sine, Ted Vaughn, Mabel Dogka, "The Elders of the Tribe" and Vincent Randall of the Yavapai-Apache Tribe of Camp Verde and Clarkdale who spent hours going over my chapters and making changes and suggestions, and to Nancy Quaid, historian for the Yavapai-Prescott Tribe, also to Louis Hood of the Fort McDowell Indian Reservation, all of whom provided encouragement and information that was invaluable.

THE YAVAPAI

The People of the Red Rocks
The People of the Sun

by
Kate Ruland-Thorne

IN THE BEGINNING

THE YAVAPAI LEGEND OF WHEN EVERYTHING BEGAN - *Ahagaskiaywa (Montezuma Well) is where the people came out first. This lake has no bottom and underneath, the water spreads out wide. When a baby is born, it is given its first bath in this sacred water.*

Long ago, there was no water in this lake. People were living down there. They lived in the inner earth with their gods, and it was a good life. But, as the anglos know, there is always a 'bad apple' in the box. They had a chief, who was a bad man and did evil things to his daughter (incest?). His daughter got mad and made him very sick. Then she made a flood and tried to kill all the people.

The chief knew he would die soon and that a great flood might come. He told the people to burn his body when he died and not let coyote get his heart. He told them to put dirt over his heart and something would grow from it.

When the chief died, the people did as they were told and corn grew up from the place where the dirt was on the chief's heart. This corn grew real big. It grew up along side of the well. When the flood came all the people including the quail, rabbits and other "people" climbed up the roots of the corn. This flood stayed level with the well.

All the ones who climbed out of the well spoke Yavapai (the Apache say they spoke Apache). But the animals wanted to exterminate the people. When the Creator heard this, he fixed it so they could no longer speak Yavapai.

After some time there was another flood, (there is only one flood in the Apache version). This happened because the people did something wrong. This flood was made of rain water. Only two people were saved in this flood...a girl and a woodpecker.

When this flood started, the people put this girl in a hollow cottonwood log. They put food in the log with her and put a small hole in it. The woodpecker made the hole in the log so she could breath.

The people told the girl to not eat all the food right away. They told her the flood would raise her up and she would hit the sky. "You will hear the noise when the log hits the sky," they said. "Just lay still, and you will get out in the end."

The girl stayed in the log 40 days and 40 nights. The girl stayed in there all the time. When the water was gone, she was in a high place people today call Sedona.

The girl came out of the log. Her name was Komwidapakwia which means, 'Old Lady White Stone.' She brought a white stone with her which protected her. She was First Woman, and the Yavapai people all come from her. She came out at Sedona where all Indians come from. It is said that her footprints were left in the wet earth (in Boynton Canyon) and those foot marks were proof that this story is so. (Present day Yavapai recall seeing these footprints, which they say were dug up and removed, possibly by archaeologists some time ago.)

Woodpecker led Komwidapokwia to a cave in a place now called Boynton Canyon. There he left her all alone. One morning she ran over to Mingus Mountain and lay down before the sun came up. When the sun came up, it hit her inside. She went to a cave where the water drips down and lay down again. The water hit her inside too. This self-insemination (virgin birth?) from the sun and purified spring water made her a baby, a little girl. (The Apache say Changing Woman had a daughter by the water, and later her daughter had a son by Father Sun.)

When the little girl came of age, her mother told her to go to the mountain and to the cave and do what she had done so they could have more people. The girl did as she was told, but the sun in the sky and the water in the cave recognized her as their daughter, so they would not go inside of her.

The girl went home and told this to her mother. Her mother said she would fix it. The mother tried many different ways to fix it, but had many problems. As a last resort, she decided to trick the sun and the water. She took her daughter back to the mountain and lay on top of her. When sun came out, he started to hit her inside, but the old lady moved over and the sun hit her daughter inside instead. She took her daughter to the cave and tricked the dripping water in the same way. This way, the girl got pregnant and had a little boy. He was called Sakarakaamche (Skara-ga-umja). The lesson in this is what women will do to get what they want. (The Apache version does not involve doing anything to "trick deities.")

When the boy was still a baby, a bad (pre-historic) eagle killed his mother. This eagle lived high on a mountain and ate anybody under him. He saw Sakarakaamche's mother gathering wild spinach one day. He grabbed her and took her to the top of his mountain and fed her to his two eaglets. So the little boy was raised by his grandmother.

In those days, there were all kinds of giant (pre-historic?) animals and they were bad. Grandmother worried that one of them would eat Sakarakaamche, just as the giant eagle had eaten his mother. Grandmother did not realize that Sakarakaamche had special medicine man power and ways given to him by the spirits. He also had great courage given to him by Father Sky, ruler of the rain, the clouds and the lightning. (The Apaches say he was sent by Grandmother to Father Sun to learn things and be tested. When he proved himself, he was given special powers to use to conquer the enemies.)

Many times, Sakarakaamche ventured out despite his grandmother's warnings and each time he would meet one of these dangerous animals. Every adventure ended with Sakarakaamche tricking then killing one of these enormous and terrible monsters. After awhile, he had killed almost

Montezuma Well - place of origin for the Yavapai and Tonto Apache. (photo by Kate Ruland-Thorne)

Montezuma Castle - ancient Sinagua dwelling, believed to be inhabited by the sacred spirits of the Gaan and the Kakaka. (photo by Kate Ruland-Thorne)

everything that was mean, cut it into pieces and scattered the pieces around. Finally all that was left was the monster eagle.

One day, Sakarakaamche asked his grandmother why he didn't have a mother. At first his grandmother would not answer and walked away. He asked all the different animals to tell him, too. But like grandmother, they were afraid that if he knew, he would be killed just like his mother was. It was a quail who finally told him the truth about his mother after Sakarakaamche had fixed his broken bones.

The quail said, "you want to know why you do not have a mother? You had a mother, but there is a bad one around...an eagle up there on that high mountain. He killed your mother."

Sakarakaamche was mad when he heard this. He went back to his grandmother and asked why she hadn't told him about his mother, and said he was going to kill that eagle. His grandmother began to cry. She told him she was afraid to tell him about the eagle because she didn't want him to be killed, too.

The young hero set out to kill the evil eagle, who soared through the heavens like a jet airplane. He knew that this monster would be the hardest of all to kill. All the little people like the dove, the mouse and the hummingbird decided to help him with this difficult task.

The dove told Sakarakaamche he must first kill the giant bull (pre-historic buffalo?) so he could use the bull's blood to trick the monster eagle. This giant bull lay on a hill between Cottonwood and Sedona, (the Apaches say they know where the exact location is even today), and every time this bull saw smoke from a campfire, he would run to it and eat everyone in sight.

Dove told Sakarakaamche to go to the river and get four weeds called okadya. He was to use them as arrows and shoot them into the four directions. These sacred arrows contained prayers that requested protection from the Four Directions. This Sakarakaamche did. The first arrow hit a pine tree and it burned. When the bull saw the fire, he ran towards it. Then the giant bull saw another pine tree burning and ran there...then another and another. Four times. Each time the bull ran away, the animals were digging a tunnel to the place where the giant bull liked to lay. All of the digger animals helped - squirrels, badgers, rats, gophers and mice. The badger was the last to make the tunnel bigger. (In Apache legend, only the gopher gets credit.)

When the bull came back, he was very tired and lay down. Mouse went into the tunnel and started to take the hair off the bull where the bull's heart was.

"What are you doing that for?" asked the bull.

"My kids are going to be cold and I want to make a bed for them with your warm fur," answered the mouse.

"All right," answered the bull, and he rolled over so the mouse could get all the fur away from where his heart was. When this was done, hummingbird hurried to get Sakarakaamche to tell him the bull was ready.

Sakarakaamche was given a red hot spear and told to go into the tunnel. All the creature people ran away because they knew what was going to happen. The young hero found the giant bull's heart right under his shoulder. He plunged the hot iron into the bull's heart, then ran back through the tunnel.

The bull had long horns and tried to kill Sakarakaamche by pushing

4

his long horns into the tunnel. But Sakarakaamche escaped unharmed just before the giant bull fell down dead.

Sakarakaamche cut the bull into many pieces and made a vest of his blood. He dipped grape leaves into the bull's blood and tied them to the vest. Then he put a handle on the vest and laid down to wait for the giant eagle to find him. (The Apaches say he crawled into the bull's stomach and covered himself with guts to cushion the eagle's drop.)

Soon the eagle came. Three times the eagle tried to get Sakarakaam-che, but the boy saw to it that the eagle missed. On the fourth try, the boy turned so the eagle could grab the handle on his vest. The boy wanted to make sure that the eagle was very tired by the fourth time.

The eagle carried him up to his nest and told his two children that he had brought them something to eat. Then he flew away to find other meat. When the baby eagles tried to eat the blood vest, Sakarakaamche whispered shhhh...this frightened them because the vest sounded rotten, so they wouldn't eat it.

Soon the giant eagle returned and asked why they hadn't eaten the food he had brought them. They said, because the food made a shhhh noise and they didn't know why. "Oh, that's because it is rotten," answered the giant eagle. The giant eagle picked Sakarakaamche up and shook him around, then threw him back on the rocks. "It's all right to eat him now," he told his children. Once again the eagle flew away.

When the children approached Sakarakaamche, he whispered shhh once more, and the children backed away. Then the boy asked the eagle children to tell him where their father sat when he came to the nest. They told him their father sat on the rim and looked around and around, then put his head under his wing and went to sleep.

"All right," said Sakarakaamche, "don't say a word when he comes back or I will kill you."

When the giant eagle returned, he sat on the rim and looked around and around, then put his head under his wing and fell asleep. As soon as he was asleep, Sakarakaamche cut the eagle's head off and threw it down the cliffs. These cliffs were so high they were half-way to the sky. Then he waited for the mother eagle to return and did the same to her. After that, he chopped off the heads of the children and threw them down the cliffs as well. It is said that you could hear the sound (thunder) for miles as each of the eagles hit the sides of the cliff.

Now with all the evil monsters dead, the young hero must find a way to get down the high, high cliffs. He sang the sacred Blackroot song, taught to him by his father, the sky. Slowly, slowly the high cliff began to go down. He saw an old woman bat gathering food below, and he called to her for help. She came to help him, but told him not to open his eyes. About 3/4's of the way down, he opened one eye, and they crashed to the ground. This broke the old bat-woman in pieces. Sakarakaamche gathered her up, and using his medicine-man power, put her back together again. She danced away, singing her gathering song. In the Apache version, "Killer of Enemies" then sets out to find his wife, who was kidnapped by Coyote.

The high, high cliffs where Sakarakaamche killed the monster eagles is now called Bell Rock, and the red mountains around Sedona are all that is left of the many monsters slain by this hero boy. It is the blood of these monsters that has caused the rocks to be red. The Apaches say *that the beads from necklaces worn by all the people who were killed by this giant eagle, can still be found scattered throughout this sacred place called Bell Rock.*

A similar verson of this Yavapai origin legend is shared by the Apache. Legends such as these could only be told on autumn and winter nights by the grandfather of the family. The origin story took four nights to tell, and the preferred place to tell the story was in a cave with a good fire burning.

Grandfather sat on one side of the fire while his audience completed the circle. Just before daylight, all the children and young men and women listening to the story were told to run to a stream and wash their face in the icy water.

"You must do this because this is a great story," said grandfather, "and if you do not, you will get crippled feet (arthritis)." This also helped create a diversion for the children.

It was dangerous to tell stories on summer nights, because spiders, bears and snakes would listen and bite the listeners. (The Apache say they are messengers who should not hear because they tell the forces who might come back to haunt you). In the winter, these creatures were hibernating, so it was a much safer time.

The Yavapai divided time into the four cycles of creation. Cycle One was when the people emerged from the underground at Montezuma Well. It terminated when a great flood welled up and covered the land.

Cycle Two was the time of the goddess Komwidapokwia (K-weden-buk-wea), "White Shell Woman" who survived the second flood and the story of her grandson, Sakarakaamche (Skara-ga-umja), the heroic monster slayer who made the world safe for all the people.

The Apache version refers to First Woman as "Changing Woman" (Echa-na-glese) and First Man, Naa-ye-nes-yane, or "Killer of Enemies".

Cycle Three was terminated by a great world fire, when Coyote stole the sun and burned up all the vegetation around the world. It was also the time when both men and animals spoke the same language, according to the Apache.

Both Apache and Yavapai consider their fourth cycle to be the present one.

"Our legends are teaching tools for the children," explains Mabel Dogka, oldest living member of the Yavapai-Apache Tribe of Clarkdale, Arizona. "They teach right and wrong, to be proud, to be strong. . .things that apply to life. When you think about these legends, you look at yourself and decide whether you are bad, good or a damn fool."

Coyote figures prominently in numerous Yavapai tales as a trickster, a wise person, or more often - a fool. The Apaches say Coyote is not wise, he only wishes he could be. Although the

Yavapai Raider - before white contact. Illustration by David Sine.

Apache and the Yavapai originate from two different language groups, they share not only a similar origin legend, but through the centuries their close proximity caused them to borrow a great deal from one another's lifeways, customs, and culture.

A STORY OF HOW THE YAVAPAI
MAY HAVE LIVED BEFORE WHITE CONTACT

Nicha stood on a rocky ledge outside his gwa'bun-yav (round house) and looked eastward into the valley below. He watched the first rays of dawn reach like crimson fingers across the horizon. In ten more dawns, his people would go on the warpath - a dream that night confirmed this.

For hours, Nicha had been awake thinking about this dream. Long after his camp had gone to sleep, he was alerted by owl that the Kakakas (ga GA gas) would pay him a visit. These dwarf-like, supernatural beings, who traveled through the air from mountain to mountain, only visited Wipukapaya's (Red rock people) who had 'medicine-power.' Nicha was one of those people. Nicha was the bamulva padje of his clan, a high man who had killed enemies with his bare hands.

Nicha fingered his medicine necklace. Necklaces such as this one were sacred, ordained by Sakarakaamche (Skara-ga-umja), First Man, in the long, long ago. Each stone on the buckskin string represented a natural power - wind, hail and rain. Nicha's fingers lingered over the most sacred stone of all - the turquoise. He loved this stone best. Because Nicha was a great warrior, a turquoise bead threaded on buckskin, also was suspended from a perforation in his nose. This symbol of honor was granted only to warriors who had performed heroic deeds and had lived at least 30 winters. Nicha was well-respected by his people.

A medicine man, now past mid-life, Nicha stood tall and lean against the rising sun. His strong, sinewy arms raised heavenward as he greeted Father Sun. Like the other men in his tribe, he wore his long hair bundled at the back of his head. All of his people wore bangs. Two eagle feathers stood upright in the back of his hair.

At the first stirring sounds of his camp awakening, Nicha directed his attention toward his hut. His stomach rumbled. He hoped his wives would start the cooking fires soon. One of them would have to help the other women tend the mescal roasting in a pit nearby. The sweet smell of its steam had permeated the air for three days and nights. Nicha's mouth watered as he thought of tasting this delicious, fibrous staple later that day. Its sweet juices always added flavor to all other food.

Suddenly a wind whipped Nicha's breech clout and raised a dust funnel. His eyes narrowed at this important omen. A whirlwind, no matter how small, signaled the passing of a ghost. Was this the spirit of a slain warrior, he wondered, one who had been killed recently by the 'Moht-Wha-ht-paya (Red-earth people)"? These traditional enemies had raided Nicha's camp several weeks before. The Kakakas told Nicha in his dream that revenge was in order, and this time the Wipukapaya would taste great victory.

Nicha thought about which young warriors he would send as a war messenger to gather other Abaya - People of the Sun - for the dance of incitement. Without this important ceremony, the raid would not be blessed. He knew he must choose warriors who could run for days without stopping, ones who knew how to find the camps of the Tolkepaya (Tolk-a-baya), 'South below people,' and the Kwevikopaya (Kwev-ka-paya) 'Elsewhere people.' These warriors must be capable of not dropping the cane crosses they would carry as they ran, crosses adorned with sacred eagle feathers. Only young warriors with the ability to speak eloquently could be chosen, ones the other clans recognized and respected because of their heroic deeds.

Nicha walked to the gwa-bun-yav of Ma'wa'tha (Bear) and told him to prepare for a long run. He must alert the Kwevikopaya who were gathering mescal in the Mazatzal Mountains. Then he awakened Gwa-gor'rda (Fox) and told him to prepare to run to the camp of the Tolkapaya who were hunting qwa-qa (deer) in the mountains of the Four Peaks. Wolf and Fox were honored to have been chosen for this important journey.

After the young warriors left, Nicha announced to his people that they must prepare for visitors. Extra gwa-bunyavs must be built and more mescal gathered and cooked in the deep pit fires. Young children were sent off with sticks to find rabbit and wood rat holes. The children were well-trained in how to route out these delicacies, and hit them with their sticks before they could get away.

Young women were sent into the woods with burden baskets strapped to their foreheads. Some would gather wild food plants and berries, others the fruit of the saguaro which was made into a refreshing drink. Still others must find more mescal, uproot it, and clean off its spiny leaves before bringing it back to bake in the fire pits.

Menstruating women, and new mothers were forbidden to scratch themselves with their fingers while the mescal was cooking, and no sexual intercourse was permitted during this important time. Otherwise the mescal might become bitter, or not be properly cooked. Only certain people, or special animals such as Nicha's dog, were permitted to light the cooking fires for the mescal.

Old warriors set to work preparing extra poison for the arrowheads to be used in the raid. Ingredients such as rattlesnake venom, spiders, centipedes, the abdominal parts of 'long-winged bees' and walnut leaves were brought forth in buckskin pouches. It took several days after these were pulverized and mixed to achieve their proper potency. After the mixture was placed in a cleaned-out deer gut, it was buried in hot ashes. A day later, it would be removed and allowed to dry. Warriors carried the poison in the bottom of their quivers. When poison was needed, they simply spread the dry mix on a flat stone, moistened it slightly, and rubbed the arrow head into the deadly concoction. A wound from such an arrowhead caused a lingering and painful death.

Grandmothers, skilled in building shelters, moved out into the lower hillsides of their mountain retreat to search for ocotilla branches. They took their granddaughters with them to help scrape the branches of spines and brace them against a circle of stones embedded in holes. Each hut was given at least three layers of thatch. The girls helped gather the grasses and sticks needed for the thatching. In this way, they learned how to build a proper hut by helping their grandmothers.

Within a few days, Bear and Wolf returned with other People of the Sun. The feasting and dancing began immediately. Warriors painted their faces black, then dipped their fingers in red pigment mixed with deer fat and marked their cheeks with red zig zags. Each painted his bangs red as well. These were the colors of war, which also served as a camouflage at night. Within days, they would attack their enemy, the 'Red-earth people,' sometime before dawn.

Nicha decided they would use war clubs on this raid, and save their poison arrows in case of actual combat. If skillful enough, combat would not be necessary. A surprise attack usually rendered their enemy helpless.

Some warriors asked permission to bring back women and children as prisoners. Nicha agreed. He knew they would be of use to the elderly ones who needed them for slaves. Booty would not to be taken. There were stringent taboos against keeping anything that belonged to the dead.

Nicha was determined to kill the mighty leader of the Red earth people. This leader's scalp could only be taken by Nicha, or another medicine man. They alone were sanctified and immune from the poison of the dead.

As Nicha's dream foretold, the People of the Sun did return victorious. Nicha carried the scalp of the enemy leader on the end of a stick, and paraded it during the victory dance. When the dance was over, Nicha threw it away.

Following the dance, the warriors joined in four days and four nights of purifying themselves in a sweat bath. During this important ceremony, none touched meat or salt. Several times each day, they washed their mouths out with soap root and yucca. By the time the purification ceremony ended, each was relieved to have been cleansed in mind, body and soul of all evil incurred during their successful raid.

Once purified, The People of the Sun returned to their designated boundaries and once gain resumed their daily routine. Mothers and wives gathered foods and medicinal plants, fathers hunted, grandfathers told the stories of the people since the time of First

Woman and First Man, grandmothers trained the children in their daily tasks, and watched over them while their parents went about their centuries-old activities.

Who are these People of the Sun? Where did they come from, and where are they today? The answers to these questions are both surprising and shocking.

WIPUKAPAYA

The People of the Red Rocks

Since ancient times, they called themselves Wipukapaya (wee-buk-abaya), 'the people of the red rock country.' The region they roamed on their hunting and plant gathering forays remains among the most lush and magnificent in the Southwest. Before white contact, the Wipukapaya were a wealthy people in terms of their environment. Unfortunately, the land that sustained them for centuries would be coveted by a more powerful and war-like tribe from the East...the English-speaking Americans.

But Americans were not the first white people the Yavapai encountered. Two hundred years before American contact, Spanish white men from Mexico entered the Verde Valley in search of fabled 'lakes of gold,' and a route to the South Seas. From 1583 until 1604, there were four separate Spanish expeditions, Espejo (1583), Farfan (1598), and Onate (1598 & 1604). Each noticed the Yavapai wearing turquoise crosses symbolizing a Dragon Fly?, a symbol that was also tatooed on their foreheads. Although these Yavapai crosses had double, horizontal bars, the Spanish assumed they were Christian crosses. They also noted in their diaries that turquoise meant gold and silver was probably nearby. Of course, this was true. A mother lode of these precious metals would eventually be discovered deep in the mountains around present-day Jerome.

The Spanish had no difficulty in recognizing the differences in language between the Yavapai and Western Apache, whom they also encountered. The Spanish referred to the Yavapai as "Niojoras," or "old - a people who have been here a long time." They also described them as 'friendly,' and the land they lived in 'full of abounding game, fertile valleys and tall pines.' The Yavapai looked upon the Spanish as 'gods' and for this reason decided it was wise to be on friendly terms with them.

The Spanish viewed the Apaches of Central Arizona in a different light. They named them 'Tonto,' which means 'crazy.' These, the Spanish decided, were a people to be feared, because they gave no quarter, and were ferocious and courageous fighters. The 'Tonto' called themselves Inde the people, and this particular sub-tribe was known as Dil-ze'e. Their two Verde Valley clans were called Chein-chii-ii (Red Rock Clan) and Yaa-go-gain (White Land Clan, named for the limestone formations of their Verde Valley home.)

11

Neither the Yavapai nor the Tonto Apache took kindly to the next white intrusion into their territory, the mountain men.

Ewing Young, accompanied by his protege, Kit Carson, was the first to trap beaver along the Salt and Verde Rivers in 1828. Although Young and his party of 75 men would gather over $20,000 worth of beaver pelts, they paid a dear price for their gain when 24 of their party were ambushed and killed by 'hostile Indians, who were either Apache or Yavapai. The mountain men didn't bother to make distinctions.

But, the Spanish explorers and the mountain men never posed unalterable threats to the lifeways of the Yavapai or Tonto Apache people. White encroachment would not became life-threatening until 1863.

Prior to that date, the Wipukapaya, (Northeastern Yavapai), roamed freely within their designated boundaries from Bill Williams Mountain to the San Francisco Peaks in Flagstaff, through Oak Creek Canyon and Sedona to the Black Hills near Jerome. They are related to two other regional Yavapai groups; the Tolkepaya, (Western Yavapai), who roamed the Bradshaw Mountains southward to the Yuma area; and the Kwevikopaya, (Southeastern Yavapai), whose area encompassed the Mazatzal, Four Peaks and Superstition Mountain region, possibly all the way to the Catalinas near Tucson. Until 1860, the combined boundaries of these three regional groups and their Tonto Apache neighbors, encompassed over 10 million square miles of territory. If any "A-baya" dared cross his boundary into the land of one of his enemies, ie: the 'Blue-green water people' (Havasupai), or the 'Red earth people' (Walapai), it was considered an open declaration of war.

Anthropologists and archaeologists do not agree on where the People of the Sun's ancestors came from. Many believe their prehistoric ancestors arrived in Central Arizona approximately 12,500 years ago during the first migration of people from Asia across the Bering Strait. They refer to these early ancestors as the Patayan, a hunting and gathering people related to the Iroquois. Others contend they are from the Hakataya cultural tradition with traits basic to all cultures with a "Yuman" root. These people come from the lower Colorado River and Lower California areas.

A variation of this concept presently being discussed suggests the Yavapai are descendants of the Southern Sinagua. This theory is supported by Yavapai oral history and legends, which contend their people lived here during the time of the huge mammoths and mastodons, giant beavers, grizzly bears, camels, horses and large bisons, animals that began to die off by 6,000 B.C.

If the A-baya were not related to the Sinagua culture, they at least co-existed peacefully alongside them. By the 1400's, however, following a 23 - year drought, archaeologists suggest they began to violently displace their pueblo neighbors after joining forces with their Apache neighbors, who had arrived in the valley in approx-

Sun Shield - Symbol of the "People of the Sun" a petroglyph commonly found at ruin sites in the Verde Valley. (photo by Hardy Quaid)

Pre-historic dwelling site near Sedona believed to be Southern Sinagua, possible ancestors to the Yavapai. (Sharlot Hall Museaum [SHM]).

imately 800 A.D.

The Apache referred to the Cliff-Dwellers as Naa-it-kede (old, or ancient people). Apache and Yavapai legends say that they lived peacefully alongside these prehistoric neighbors, but trouble arose after the Cliff-Dwellers stole their property. This resulted in warfare which forced the Cliff-Dwellers to move to the Salt River Valley. Eventually these people became known as the Pima and Papago, and forever afterwards were considered the traditional enemies of the Yavapai and Apache tribes.

Both the Yavapai and Apache share the origin story which pinpoints exactly where their people came from - Montezuma Well near Sedona. It was here, they say, that First Woman emerged after the Great flood. Following a virgin birth, her grandson, First Man was born and grew up to battle huge, pre-historic monsters (mammoths?) in order to make the land safe for all The People who followed.

Modern ethnologists document the Yavapai as a Yuman-speaking group whose ancestral cousins are the Mojave, Yuma, Cocopa, Walapai, Havasupai, and Maricopa people. The Yavapai befriended and sometimes intermingled with their later-arriving Western Apache neighbors, in particular the Yaa-go-gain Clan. After both tribes were forced to move to the San Carlos Reservation in the 1870s, intermarriage was even more frequent. As a result, it was mistakenly assumed the Yavapai belonged to this linguistically Athabascan group.

"The Apache came here to this land after we did," explained 86 year-old Mabel Dogka, the oldest living member of the Yavapai and Apache tribe. "We mixed with them. That's how we became known as Yavapai-Apache." Mabel's own mother was a Tonto Apache and her father was a Yavapai.

The reservation where Mabel grew up includes portions of Camp Verde (established in 1904) and Clarkdale (1969) in the Verde Valley. In the early days, her people wintered in caves, but switched to brush-covered wikiups. . .or "teepee houses" as Mabel Dogka calls them, during warmer months. She remembers living in a wikiup as a child.

"When I was a little girl, I remember white people saying, 'why do those people have haystacks everywhere'?" They thought our houses were haystacks.

Prior to the arrival of the white people, the Yavapai and Tonto Apaches easily roamed within the boundaries of their territory in search of ripening plant products and game. There were cordial relations, and on rare occasions, intermarriage between the Wipukapaya and the Ah-why-gas (Yavapai word for Tontos). Not only did these Yavapai and Apache groups sometimes intermarry, but they hunted and gathered freely across one another's boundaries, and often cooperated in war.

In the Sedona and the Verde Valley, the two bands which were

Ancient Yavapai Petroglyphs near Sedona. Photos by Kate Ruland-Thorne.

made up entirely of Apache and Yavapai were the Red Rock Clan (Che'in chii ii) and the White Land Clan (Yaa go gain). These people intermarried over several generations. The Yaa go gain were located along the Mogollon Rim, and Red Rock Clan boundries were Oak Creek, Dry Beaver Creek and Wet Beaver Creek and southward to the west side of the Verde River.

It is interesting to note that the Yavapai and the Apache in these two bands maintained their own distinctive language and identity. The children from these mixed-marriages simply became bilingual, and identified their descent through their mother. Therefore, the child of a Yavapai mother and Apache father was considered a Yavapai.

Among the Apache and Yavapai, war was a well planned affair, usually precipitated by a dream. The warrior's medicine man predicted the happenings to come through his dreams. Very few activities were initiated without 'dream power.'

Rarely did the Yavapai or Apache kill a blood relative or clan member. Such an act was looked upon with horror. It would be like taking vengence upon one's self, they believed. Only if a relative or clan member committed the most heinous crime of all - incest, was such a killing excusable.

The topic of incest was avoided entirely in the belief that it, and all irregular sex practices between members of the opposite sex were linked to witchcraft, which made it all the more repulsive. Anyone caught in such acts was marked for life and ostracized. Families remained very tight-knit in cases like this. The most repugnant of all incestuous relationships were between a father and daughter, or brother and sister, and considered much worse than between blood or clan relatives. In these cases, the culprits were put to death.

It was everyone's duty to look after one another's children. Killing or abusing one's child was the ultimate act of brutality and another inexplicable abnormality. Considering modern day anglo news stories that are rife with such practices, it seems our highly touted 'civilized' society could gain greatly by studying the historical mores of these 'primitive' folk.

The usual purpose behind raiding and warfare was to avenge the death of a kinsman. The Yavapai did not take booty after a raid as the Apache customarily did, because they believed they might be haunted by the dead person's personal effects. The taking of booty in the Apache mind, was all part of the revenge. After white contact, booty, in particular guns and livestock, became the primary reason behind raids by both the Yavapai and Apache. By the mid 1800s, these items signified wealth. Revenge took on greater meaning by then as well.

The other hated enemies of the Tonto and all three Yavapai groups were the Pima and Maricopa tribes. Together, (or separately), the Yavapais and Apaches often made vicious raids upon the Pima,

Maricopa, Havasupai and Walapai...and visa-versa. All of this warring and raiding accelerated their eventual downfall when in the 1870's, General George Crook took clever advantage of these old animosities and employed peaceful Indians as Scouts to help him hunt down and subdue those he considered "hostiles.".

There are no known oral histories of war taking place between the Yavapai and their neighbors, the Navajo and Hopi. With these tribes, the Yavapai were cordial, and carried on a lucrative and beneficial trading activity. The Hopi and Navajo people particularly valued the finely tanned deer and antelope hides of the Yavapai, which they readily traded for their own highly prized blankets. Three Navajo or Hopi blankets was a common price for one tanned Yavapai buckskin.

The Apache, however, had periodic run-ins with the Navajo, their Athabascan-speaking cousins. Whenever the Apache went to Hopi to trade, they crossed the high desert at night in order to avoid any conflict with them.

Traditionally, the Yavapai hunted qwa-qa (deer) before daylight. Hunters were barred from sexual intercourse for two days prior to the hunt in order to conserve strength for the long distances they had to run. Runners with the greatest endurance were sent out to track the deer. Often this took all day. Eventually, the deer were driven into a line of men who surrounded them in a narrow canyon and killed them with bows and arrows.

Other times, runners decoyed the deer by blowing on a piece of grass in their mouth. This whistling sound imitated the cry of a fawn. A lone hunter might wear a stuffed deer head while he stalked the deer. When the stalker came upon a buck, he angered it by striking the horns of his mask against a bush or tree. When the buck charged, the hunter shot him with a bow and arrow. After rifles were introduced, the deer-head mask was seldom used.

The hunter skinned his deer from chin to anal opening, then down the inside of each leg. Once removed, the hide was waved toward the east for good luck. No part of the deer was thrown away. Its brains were preserved by cooking it in ashes, and spread over grass where it dried into a cake-like substance. Brains were essential for tanning the hide. Every portion of the animal's body had a particular use and purpose. All buckskin clothing was made by the men of the tribe, and their skill in tanning hides was widely acclaimed. Many rolls of buckskin showed that a man was a good hunter and that his family was wealthy.

Most of the garments worn by the Yavapai and Apache people were made from these supple hides, fashioned by the men with deer-bone awls and sinew thread. In warm weather, a buckskin breechcloth and knee or hip-high moccasins were the only attire worn by the men. The Apache's knee-length moccasins were distinctive because they had flap that went up over their big toes, which protected them on long runs.

Yavapai and Apache women were required to be more modest. They wore two pieces of buckskin. The piece in front was worn like a butcher's apron, suspended by "spaghetti string" type straps that hung from shoulders to ankles. The back piece hung from the waist down and was tied with a belt. These sleeveless dresses were fringed along the sides, and worn both winter and summer. A Navajo or Hopi blanket served as a warm cape when the weather turned cold. Moccasins for both men and women usually reached to their knees. Children wore nothing at all in the summer months until they turned nine or ten years old.

After her first menses, a young woman was tattooed on her arm, chin and forehead with cactus needles and charcoal pigment. Her mother was never allowed to perform this delicate operation. Meat eating was forbidden until the tattoo healed. Men were tattooed as well.

Mabel Dogka's face and arm were tattooed in this manner when she was a young girl. "This is a clan design, and if you are Apache, it shows which clan you belong to," explained Mabel. All Wipukapaya used tattoo marks to identify themselves.

Eyelids of both sexes were painted black with a stick. Women painted their faces with white earth for certain sacred dances. During the hottest part of the summer, both sexes painted their faces red to prevent sunburn.

The Yavapai and Apache used red mineral pigments (from hemetite, or iron ore) on their faces for social dances as well. The whole face was painted red and decorated with zig-zagging lines scraped by three fingers down the cheeks.

Warriors sometimes painted their hair white before war. Red paint mixed with deer fat, or the bone marrow of the deer, kept the faces of all ages warm and free of chapping in winter. It served as an excellent, primitive 'cold cream.'

Boys 10 to 12 were required to run in winter mornings with a snowball under their armpits in order to prevent the growth of axillar hair. This helped them become 'strong men.' Boys were instructed to drink water only in the morning and evening in order to train them to go without water while hunting or on the war-path. Another endurance lesson required young boys to run to the top of a mountain or hill without stopping. Growing boys were not fed much in order to toughen them for abstinence on long journeys. Most of the young boy's training was done by grandparents or the elders of the clan who tried to prepare him for the harshness of life. A boy was not considered a man until he was at least 25 to 30 years old. A 'man' was one who could shoulder responsibilities. If he was particularly wise, or had reached an 'age of wisdom,' he was automatically referred to as a Ba-yan. This was a term he could not convey upon himself. Only others who admired his wisdom could decide to refer to him in this way.

Mabel Dogka's gwa-bun-ya-v (Apaches say ko-wa), or "teepee

house," was not carried from place to place as the people traveled, but freshly built at each new camp. At traditional campsites, to which the people returned each season, the old homes simply required a new cover. Otherwise, it took one person a full day to build a new hut. The openings to the hut always faced East. When someone died, the hut and all the belongings were burned to the ground. This was done to keep the dead person's spirit from staying around, and to free it to go on to the next world. The dead person's name was not mentioned again thereafter.

The people cooked their food by either boiling it in pots, or in pitched baskets buried in a rock hole. Often they roasted it on hot coals and ashes, or cooked it in 'earth ovens'(bar-b-que pits). Baked mescal, gathered in April and May, was frequently eaten at each meal. Meat was dipped in its hot, sweet juice.

In order to uproot the mescal, (agave or Century plant), the women and children used a digging stick which was driven beneath the mescal with a stone. Once the plant was turned upside down, its thick spiny leaves were cut off with a hunting knife. Each family would dig and trim about a dozen plants and carry them to camp in their burden baskets. Not just any plant was dug out, much trial and error was involved in finding the sweetest ones. Also, the people knew not to clear-cut an area. Always some plants were left, so that they might grow and feed them again.

The agave heads were cooked in a fire (or bar-b-que) pit dug four feet deep in the ground. Placed on top of hot stones, the agave was then covered with a thick coating of grass and earth. Cooking of the mescal began at noon and lasted until dawn of the second or third day. It was pounded into cakes and wrapped in wet buckskin.

Mabel Dogka remembers eating mescal as a child and enjoying it. "When it's first removed from the fire-pit, it is sweet like candy," she recalls. "After you peel it, you have to chew it, because it has lots of fiber. It's like eating sugar cane. After it dries and hardens, it can make your tongue raw if you chew it too long. My people don't even know what mescal is anymore," she adds.

"I remember, as a child, getting rabbits out of a hole," she continued. "We'd all stand around (these were usually group hunts) with sticks. When the rabbit tried to run, we were supposed to hit it with our sticks. I remember I would just holler and couldn't hit it. My parents got after me for that. We did the same with wood rats. We stole from them, too. They packed a lot of pinions in their burrow, and we would take these nuts from them. Sometimes we ran into rattlesnakes doing that."

Snakes were not eaten by either the Yavapai or Apache people, nor were frogs, turtles, fish, ducks or geese . . .or anything that smelled fish-like. These taboos were given to them by the ancients. Large black and yellow caterpillars, and wasp nests were considered a delicacy, however.

19

Although primarily a hunting and gathering people, the Yavapai and Apache did cultivate corn, squash and beans. Tobacco, which grew wild, was gathered as well. Men were not allowed to smoke tobacco until they were over 40 years old. The legend the Yavapai tell about tobacco is that it was once a very beautiful woman, jilted by a young man. In order to spite him, she turned into tobacco so that all men would desire her forever.

The Gaan (Ga-han), a class of supernatural beings, are the sacred people who possess the power of the Great Spirit Himself. They are equivalent to the Hopi Katchina, and the Navajo Yei, and revered as a significant religious figure by both Yavapai and Apache people.

It is believed that the Gaan were builders of certain prehistoric ruins, and still are the inhabitants of specific mountains and cave sites. Presently, these sacred sites include the Four Peaks area and Montezuma Castle, among others. They share the San Francisco Peaks with the spirits of the Hopi Kachinas and the Navajo Yei. Like the Hopi and Navajo mythological tales, the Gaan are believed to still live on earth as spirits. They are called upon to help during times of war, sickness and death, or special ceremonies. They once were a people who left because of disrespect and went in search of places where eternal life could be lived without evil things.

Because a Gaan is a spirit, he has no known face. When the Crown Dancers imitate him, they wear masks with eyes only. This is because these spirits might be a relative from the past - or now. The Apaches do not share this belief, but consider the Gaan deities.

Yavapai legends claim that their people learned about the Gaan from the Kakaka, or 'little Indians.' (The Apache learned about the Gaan from the Almighty, they say). The Kakaka are known to have dwelled in all sacred ruin sites throughout the Verde Valley. The doors of the ruins were designed for a very 'small' Indian. It was the Kakaka who taught the Yavapai all their dances and songs, had the power to foretell the future, and to heal the sick. They often left important messages on the stones (petroglyphs). (These little Indians were like the wind. They could not be seen but their presence was felt in the movement of the clouds, bushes, grass and trees, etc.) They only communicated with the medicine men. When times were difficult, or someone was terribly ill, it was common for the medicine man to gather all the people together to pray for help from the Kakaka.

Even today, these little Indians are never spoken about by the traditional believers among the Yavapai or Apache. To speak of them with non-believers is bad luck. If anyone ever sees a Kakaka, they can be assured they will soon experience their own, or someone elses - death. An exceptionally good, modern day medicine man is still capable of summoning the spirits of these little Indians for help during sacred healing sings.

We know the most significant legend shared by all three Yavapai groups, as well as the Apache, is the legend of their origin from the depths of Montezuma Well. All land surrounding this ancient limestone sink, which extends throughout present-day Sedona to Boynton Canyon, is considered very holy ground, not only by the Yavapai and Apache, but by the Navajo and Hopi people as well.

WHITE MAN COMES

Almost two centuries would pass between the last Spanish 'entrada' into the Verde Valley and the arrival of the gold-seeking Americans. It was the Army who first labeled the Yavapai - 'Mohave-Apache.' Perhaps it was because the Yavapai introduced themselves as A-baya, which sounds somewhat like 'Apache,' or because the language spoken by both the Yavapai and their 'cousins' the Mohave was very similar. Whatever the reason, this misunderstanding, deliberate or otherwise, became the root cause of unspeakable hardships and suffering for the People of the Sun from that time forward.

Following on the heels of the gold-hungry prospectors were the settlers. Together, they insisted on protection from the 'Apache.' By 1864, the U.S. Army was building forts throughout Yavapai and Apache ancestral lands.

Initially the Yavapai made every effort to remain on friendly terms with these new interlopers. The chiefs among the Yavapai sent messengers to all their people telling them, "don't fight the white people. If you fight them, more and more will come. They are like water, like ants. They have an ant hill back where the sun comes up. You can't stop them." The chiefs promised the whites they would not fight, but would rather live among them peacefully. But Yavapai land was too rich to share with such a 'primitive people.' In less than 10 years, white efforts to destroy the well-ordered lifeways of the Yavapai and the Apache, and exterminate them as a people, very nearly succeeded.

The end of the war between the states marked the beginning of drastic changes for the Yavapai people, who lived in the heart of what was to become 'gold-rush country.' For the first time they faced a foe more deadly than any imagined, even in their most frightening legends.

In 1864, new recruits, together with hundreds of seasoned veterans, enlisted to fight new foes - the American Indians of the West. Government policy at that time was to subdue, and if necessary exterminate, all tribes who impeded Western settlement and industry.

Soldiers knew that fighting the fierce Apaches of Arizona and New Mexico, required particular skill and heroic fearlessness. For many, the challenge was irresistible. Unfortunately, the peace-seeking Yavapai of Arizona were mistaken for Apaches. . .or, as the Yavapai tell it. . .there was no mistake.

"Calling the Yavapai 'Apache' was a very convenient excuse for the

---

21

English speaking Americans to kill the Yavapai and take over our land. The Apache fought with guns when the white people wanted to push them out of their lands. So the white people considered them their worst enemies. 'Apache' meant the same as enemies to them. Anyone called Apache could be killed, they said. And the Yavapai were also 'Apache' to them. We Yavapai had no guns. We had only bow and arrow and club. We knew we could not fight army guns with a bow and arrow and club. So our chiefs promised the white people we would not fight with them. But the Yavapai land contained lots of gold and copper and other valuable metals. The land was good for cattle ranching. Along the rivers and springs, there was good land for farming. The white people wanted that land for themselves alone, and the Indians out. By calling the Yavapai 'Apache' they felt it was only all right to kill us and push us off our land."
(THE YAVAPAI OF FORT MCDOWELL - No.701 History Grant of U.S Dept. of Housing and Urban Development).

Well respected Arizona historians support this contention. "The Yavapais were not immediately hostile to the Americans entering their country, but in the early 1860's with the discovery of gold in the region, large numbers of miners and settlers began to move into the valleys prized by the Yavapai as hunting grounds, and after 1865, the white population grew rapidly. When the first clash occurred between the Indians and the aggressive Americans is not certain, but it appears that attacks against the Yavapai were begun by American miners as early as 1860." (SMOKE SIGNAL, 1964 by Sidney" Brinkerhoff - author and Assistant Director for Museums at the Arizona Pioneer's Historical Society).

"The recent discovery of gold near the San Francisco Mountains within the District of Northern Arizona, and the flocking thither of many citizens of the United States, renders it necessary that a small military force should be sent to these new gold fields to protect miners from the Indians." (SMOKE SIGNALS," 1972 - Quoted from General James Carlton, commander of the Department of New Mexico in his 1863 General Order –27 by author and historian, Andrew Wallace of N.A.U. who added, "Nothing was said about protecting the Indians from the miners.") It is also worth noting that no gold has ever been found in the San Francisco Mountains. Carlton probably meant Granite Mountain near Prescott.

Between 1865 and 1875, the population of Arizona's 6,000 Yavapai people was reduced to less than 1,000. What follows is a description of signifcant events beginning in 1860 and ending in 1875 which unveils a pattern that strongly supports the premise that hate and greed provoked vicious wars between the Yavapai, Apaches and the Americans, wars which inflicted untold misery and death upon both sides and very nearly exterminated the Western Apache, and the People of the Sun - forever.

THE INDIAN WARS OF NORTH CENTRAL ARIZONA

Told from the Indian's point of view

"Just now our red brethren are awful thick hearabouts. They are seen in the woods, close to town, in the rocks below town, on Granite Creek. . .in fact everywhere. So keep your powder dry and whenever you see an Indian that says, 'Americano mucho bueno. . .' kill him; he don't mean it." (Arizona Miner, July 27," 1867)

22

*Yavapai warrior with owl
feather head dress, 1800s.
(Fort Verde State Park
[FVSP])*

*King Woolsey, Rancher, miner
and early day Indian fighter. [SHM]*

How The West Was Won - Gattling gun at Fort McDowell, c 1890s. [SHM]

Gold fever! Like a seductive femme fatale, it enticed sane, hard working men into the realm of debauchery and madness. Many abandoned their farms, businesses - their whole way of life - just for the sight of this yellow harlot. Her lure caused men to either abandon, or worse, drag their entire families across mountains and deserts, into the unknown where unspeakable dangers, hardship, and often death was their only reward.

With each new discovery, another 'rush' was on. Beginning in 1849, the rush was first to 'Californey,' then to 'Colorady' and by 1863, it was off to 'Arizoney' with a wash pan on my knee.

"If ya stumble on a rock, don't kick it - cash it," was one popular phrase of the time. And, "If ya wash yer face in the Hassayampa River, you kin pan four ounces of gold dust from yer whiskers," claimed others.

Ironically the ones who built the greatest fortunes during this incredible era of greed, were rarely the prospectors. It was the prostitutes, the gamblers, the outlaws, the merchants who supplied goods to the gold and silver camps, and the financiers who sat safely in their plush offices and grubstaked any prospector with a good ore sample in his poke.

The little guy who faced all the dangers, did all the digging and made the discoveries and sacrifices, was lucky if he ended up with the shirt on his back and his scalp still in tact. But even when it was obvious that this 'fever' could be fatal, it was no deterrent to the next rush of prospectors who followed.

In the beginning, only one factor blunted the plundering of the gold fields of North-Central Arizona. This was known as "Apache Land," a dreaded place where death lurked behind every rock, cactus and tree. Of the few who attempted to settle in its vast realm prior to 1860, none succeeded and few returned. The Apache and the Yavapai were its complete masters until the beginning of the 1860s. After the first serious intrusions into their heartland, the Indians discovered they shared only one common purpose with these white intruders - a desire to completely exterminate the other. . .and the war was on.

The Indian people of North Central Arizona had their initial warning of a possible white invasion following the Mexican War and the Treaty of Guadalupe Hidalgo in 1848. Until then, only a handful of mountain men knew anything about their lands, which were acquired from Mexico following this treaty.

Desirous to learn possible routes for wagons, railroads and steamboats through this unknown region, the U.S. Government carefully selected a group of West Point engineers, whom they called the Army Corps of Topographical Engineers, to explore, survey and map this territory. Sitgraeves, Beal and Whipple, all members of this elite corps, would be among those who left an indelible stamp upon the face of Northern Arizona and the Verde Valley. . .an area marked by a line known as the 35th Parallel. This 35th Parallel ran like a dagger through the heart of Yavapai and Apache country.

Based on an interview with mountain man Joseph Walker (who would play a significant role later in North Central Arizona), Capt. Lorenzo Sitgreaves was the first of these scientist-explorers to set out from the Zuni Villages in New Mexico in 1851 and cross through Indian country. During his 650 mile trek, Sitgreaves and his expedition of 20 men, an escort of soldiers, and his guide, mountain man Antoine Leroux, suffered from two savage attacks, one by the Yavapais and the other by Yuma Indians. They finally arrived at Fort Yuma on the Colorado River, starving and barely alive. Despite their harrowing escapes, Sitgreaves and his crew managed to map an area that had previously been considered Terra Incognita.

By 1853, Lt. Amiel W. Whipple was sent on a similar expedition which traversed approximately the same area. Before he left, Whipple interviewed a French-Canadian explorer, Francois X. Aubrey, who claimed to have led a wagon train along the 35th Parallel a few months before. Aubrey told a tale of encountering Indians who used rifle balls made of gold, and who traded large quantities of gold for an old mule and some clothes. His story spread like the desert wind across the Southwest to the eager ears of gold-hungry prospectors in California and Colorado.

Despite several shoot-outs with the Yavapais, Aubrey convinced Whipple that the 35th Parallel was the best route for a future railroad, and the Indians along the way were not in sufficient numbers, and could be subdued. By Christmas of 1853, Whipple, his assistant Lt. Joseph Ives, and their crew were camped at the foot of the San Francisco Peaks in the middle of a severe snowstorm.

At the head waters of the Verde River's West Fork, the Whipple expedition turned south and headed toward the Bill Williams Fork on the Colorado, then northwest to the coast of California. Whipple's meticulous survey confirmed that a railroad could be built through Northern Arizona to California, and his maps and reports provided invaluable information for the future developers of the Santa Fe Railroad and eventually, Interstate 40.

Edward Fitzgerald Beal would be the first to build an actual wagon road across Northern Arizona in 1859. His expedition was perhaps the most unique of all. Beal imported camels as his beasts of burden. But due to the outbreak of the Civil War in 1860, Beal's famous road would not be used until several years later.

Despite Whipple's well-marked map and Beal's first wagon road, the whisperings of fortunes in gold in northern Arizona was still not enough to inspire the hoards of prospectors who usually stopped at nothing. "Them injuns is jest too fearsome in Arizony," most concluded. It would take mountain men like Joseph Walker and Pauline Weaver, men who were more Indian than white, to confirm that there was plenty of gold to be found in 'Arizony,' enough to make the dangers pale by comparison.

Unfortunately for the Yavapai and the Tonto Apaches, the first great bonanzas of this precious metal would be discovered throughout their ancestral lands by these very same mountain men.

In 1861, one of America's great pathfinders, Joseph Walker, led an expedition of 18 prospectors into northern Arizona with the hopes of finding gold around the San Francisco Peaks. Having no luck, and with cold weather setting in, the Walker party continued on to Santa Fe to sit out the winter. There he met Gen. James Carleton, military commander of New Mexico.

Carleton, who had led the successful California Volunteers during the early stage of the Civil War against Southern intrusions into the Southwest, was obviously well acquainted with the reports of the potential gold fields in North-Central Arizona. He very likely had also heard the tales of Indians using golden bullets and wearing ornaments made of gold. Surely he too had been affected by 'the fever' because by the time he met the Walker party, he was ready to share some vital information.

To Walker's great advantage, Carleton directed him to return to Arizona and head straight to an area later known as the Bradshaw Mountains near present day Prescott. Carleton sent along his friend, Albert Benedict, also a member of his California Volunteers, to insure his own interests in any possible mining claims. We know that by 1864, following the Walker Party's great discoveries in the Bradshaws, Benedict was 'overseeing Carlton's mining claims in the area.'

The Walker Party began placer mining near Granite Mountain, Lynx, Turkey and Big Bug Creeks in February of 1863. By May 10, they hit the first of the major 'Mother Lodes' and established the Pioneer Mining District. The gold rush was on to 'Arizony.'

By June 25 of that same year, the Weaver Mining District was established in traditional Yavapai land. Immediately, General Carleton saw to it that the capital of Arizona Territory was moved from Tucson to Prescott, making it the only wilderness capital in United States history.

In his report on the strike at the Walker Mining District, Capt. N. Pishon, First Regiment, Cavalry, California Volunteers, reported to his commanding officer, Brig. Gen. James Carlton: "The new government of Arizona, if it ever will come, will be at the new gold fields, not at the insignificant village of Tucson." As a result, Carlton was motivated to establish Fort Whipple, from which the town of Prescott sprang, on October 23, 1863. "By General Order –27, I hereby establish the Military District of Northern Arizona," wrote Carleton. One can only suspect that his motivation was just a little self-serving.

The Weaver Mining District came next. It was named after the famous mountain man, Indian scout and explorer, Pauline Weaver. Weaver claimed to be half Cherokee. He was a member of the Ewing Young trapping party, which included Kit Carson, when they trapped along the Salt and Verde Rivers in 1831.

26

Weaver was the first to hit a bonanza of gold on the Colorado River, which initiated the western boom towns of La Paz and Ehrenberg. Concerned about what was happening to his Indian friends during the Arizona gold rush, Weaver taught them the password, "Pauline Tobacco." Early settlers knew that when an Indian used that password, they were friendly Indians. This saved many lives on both sides at first. But, newcomers ignored the password. Their attitude was: "Injuns is injuns, and the only good 'uns is dead 'uns." Eventually Weaver was accidentally attacked by a Yavapai war party in 1867, and wounded. He managed to crawl to Fort Lincoln (later renamed Fort Verde) where he died, some say of malaria and others of the wounds. When the Yavapai learned what they had done, they were deeply sorry and for months afterwards inquired daily about their friend 'Paulino.' The final words written on his tombstone were: "His greatest achievement was as peacemaker between races."

Another man who played a prominent role in gold seeking and the Indian wars was King Woolsey. He reportedly joined up with the Walker Party when they established the first mining district in Central Arizona.

King Woolsey was one of the first to mine along Lynx Creek in the heart of Yavapai country. His ranch, which he homesteaded on the Agua Fria River, provided refuge for many settlers during the Indian wars in Central Arizona.

Gov. P.K. Safford, third territorial governor, designated Woolsey, whom he considered "a prominent citizen of the territory, rancher and owner of several mines," as one others might look to in times of trouble. Woolsey organized citizen volunteers for repeated expeditions against the 'hostiles' and gained fame and popularity as a successful Indian fighter.

The press announced in 1860 that Woolsey led a party of 100 men to prospect for gold, silver and 'copper-colored wretches.' Without exception, these volunteers sought vengeance. The barbarism of one member of the group in particular, Sugarfoot Jack, was so horrifying it even shocked Woolsey.

On several occasions, Sugarfoot Jack tossed crying Indian babies into the flames of burning wickiups during raids, and on one occasion, bounced a screaming toddler on his knee until it stopped crying. When the baby finally smiled at him, he shot it in the face. Nevertheless, Woolsey's comment on the subject of Indians was, "I choose to fight the broad platform of extermination."

Another famous member of the Walker Party who joined in the effort to exterminate Indians in order to preserve his own mining interests was Jack Swilling. Swilling owned several rich mines in Yavapai country. As a member of the famous Walker Party, he too was among the first to discover gold in the Bradshaw Mountains.

A former Confederate officer, Union Scout and "all around hellion," Swilling organized the Swilling Irrigation Company in

27

1867. His company set to work cleaning out ancient Hohokam canals leading to the Salt River. As a result, farmers once again made the desert bloom with crops, and the city of Phoenix eventually was born.

Swilling bore wounds from his numerous shoot-outs with Indians. These caused him great pain and eventually he succumbed to morphine and whiskey in his later years. He died in Yuma Prison in 1878, accused of a crime he did not commit.

From September to December of 1863, three more mining districts were established in the heart of Yavapai country, and by 1867, over 8,000 mining claims had been recorded in this same district. Indian raids and depredations increased. In order to deal more effectively with their Indian problems, the citizens of Prescott joined in what later became known as the infamous "Pinole Massacre."

In early January of 1864, the Yavapai and Pinal Mountain Apaches were invited to a "peace feast" in which all the food for the Indians was poisoned. Thirty-six Indians died. This affair also has been referred to as the "Incident at Bloody Tanks." It is an event which has attracted considerable attention through the years. Those who participated, defended their actions for the rest of their lives. Charles Poston, a pioneer and Arizona Territory's first Superintendent of Indian Affairs, explained that King Woolsey (who was in charge of his volunteers during this escapade) saw at once that either the Americans or the Indians were to be slaughtered, so he said, "Boys, we have got to die or get out of this." According to Poston, who defended Woolsey's actions, "they proceeded to do the latter by poisoning the Indian's food."

A conflicting report states that the food was not poisoned, the Indians were simply shot outright during the 'peace negotiations.' Regardless of how they were actually killed, the Yavapai realized they had little choice but to join with the Apaches in their war against the whites.

By February 2, one month after the Pinole Massacre, Yavapai Chief Qua-shac-a-ma warned Indian Agent Bennett against any more white encroachment on Yavapai lands.

The Chief told Bennett that white people had come into his country and taken some of the best planting places and told his people not to plant there any more. These whites had also driven all the game out and now his people were starving. The Chief's warnings were ignored and by March 3, the Yavapai began attacking ranches and driving off stock in order to survive.

On April 11, King Woolsey, his volunteers along with soldiers from Ft. Whipple retaliated by attacking Yavapai rancheras. By now, Woolsey had launched his second major expedition of citizens, (mostly miners numbering 100 men, with the view of not only making war on the Indians, but also exploring potential mining sites.) That same month, N.H. Davis, Assistant Inspector General of the U.S. Army, informed General Carlton that Woolsey was a man well fitted to lead companies of miners against the "Apaches."

By June 1, King Woolsey led yet another expedition against the Yavapai, this time against Delchay, a major war chief. Also known as "Big Rump," Delchay was often labeled a Tonto Apache, but was in fact a Yavapai. During his time he became as notorious a renegade as Geronimo.

In September of that same year, Captain John Moss succeeded in making a treaty with the Yavapai to keep trails and roads free from their hostile raids. The following month, a memorandum was sent to the U.S. Congress requesting $150,000 to place Arizona Indians on reservations.

"From 1864, the army began building camps and forts throughout Yavapai country. The army wanted the Yavapai to settle in reservations around these forts. They told the Yavapai they would give them food, cloths, horses, cattle wagons and houses. First the Yavapai believed them and went to Camp Date Creek and Fort McDowell. But when the people were there, they found they did not get what the white people promised them. There was very little and poor food. The soldiers abused their women, shot their men and gave them terrible diseases. Many of the Tolkopaya (McDowell people) died from small pox after they had been given infected clothes. So the Yavapai did not want to live on these reservations and left." (THE YAVAPAI OF FORT MCDOWELL).

On September 26, 1864, the First Territorial Legislature met in Prescott. King Woolsey, at 32 years of age, became the second youngest member of the legislative council. He was made chairman of Militia and Indian Affairs as well as being appointed to other committees on Finance, Agriculture and the Judiciary. He also successfully voted to make Henry W. Fleury, a self-proclaimed atheist, "chaplain" of the legislative body.

The most pressing concern before this first legislative session was the need for troops to make war against the "Apaches." Although there was a shortage of governmental funds, lawmakers appropriated $1487.00 to reimburse Woolsey and others for their expeditions against the Apaches. By now, both Yavapai and Apaches were considered one and the same.

On May 20, 1865, the Yavapai again made an effort to live in peace with the white population. Twenty-seven of them agreed to work on the Ft. Mohave Toll Road under the 'protection' of Superintendent of Indian Affairs, G.W. Leihy. All 27 Yavapai were attacked and shot down by soldiers from Ft. Whipple.

Four months later, the Yavapai joined forces with the Mohave and Yuma tribes (their linguistic cousins) in a war against Piutes and Chemehuevi Indians in retaliation for their serving as army scouts.

Peace talks were once again initiated on April 13, 1866 between the Yavapai and the military. This time, a Yavapai band under Chief

Echa-waw-cha-comma (Hitting the Enemy), met the soldiers near Grapevine Springs in Skull Valley for purpose of this treaty. Troops from Ft. Whipple ambushed them, killing 30 Yavapai and wounding 40, despite the fact that Echa-waw-cha-comma traveled to this meeting with a note from Superintendent of Indian Affairs, Leihy, granting his band immunity.

"East of Prescott is Skull Valley. It is called that way because people found many bones and skulls scattered throughout that place. These bones and skulls were from Yavapai. The soldiers called Yavapai from all over to this place. They told them they would give them wagons and horses and many other good things if they came to this place. When the Yavapai arrived, the soldiers started shooting them. Some of the Yavapai escaped and told others about it. But most of them got killed and were left lying there. Skull Valley is called after the skulls of the Yavapai." (from THE YAVAPAI OF FORT MCDOWELL).

Four months later, 100 Yavapai attacked the army at Grapevine Springs in Skull Valley, but were repelled after 45 minutes of fighting. Later that same month, the Yavapai took control of the country around Skull Valley. They ordered the whites out and charged a toll on livestock and goods going over the roads.

These toll roads had been established because the First Territorial Legislature knew they could not afford to build wagon roads. They authorized a half dozen toll roads which they hoped would span the territory. It was one of these vital toll roads that the Yavapai had seized. The following month, on November 10, Superintendent of Indian Affairs, G.W. Leihy and his clerk were killed by the Yavapai at Bell Canyon near Prescott.

Special Order #16 established a military camp and reservation along Date Creek on January 23, 1867, to be named Camp McPherson. The post was later re-named, Camp Date Creek.

"Maj. Gen. Henry W. "Old Brains" Halleck directed that a permanent military camp be founded on Date Creek and named for Gen. J.B. Mc Phearson, killed in the battle of Atlanta in 1864. Halleck picked this location because of its strategic location in the heart of Yavapai country, 60 miles from Prescott, and less than 30 miles from Wickenburg. Settlers lived along the banks of this creek, miners prowled the surrounding mountains, and to the north were the ranchers in Skull Valley. Also, the main stage and freight road from La Paz on the Colorado River to Prescott ran near, and crossed this creek." (Sidney Brickerhoff - THE SMOKE SIGNAL - Fall 1964)

Two months after the establishment of this reservation, the Yavapai attacked a wagon train eight miles west of Camp Date Creek, which prompted a military troop to pursue them and launch a surprise attack on them in Hell's Canyon. Several days later, this same troop under Capt. Williams and the 8th Cavalry attacked and destroyed 30 Apache lodges in the Black Hills. Williams and his troops engaged the Apaches in a running battle near the Verde

River, followed by two other battles in the Black Mountains. Throughout the summer and into the fall, raids and battles between citizens, the army and the enraged Indians continued at a relentless pace.

Before the year was over, Gen. Gregg and the Yavapai met to explore peace proposals once again. Due to poor interpreters, the peace efforts failed.

Gen. Gregg, a dashing senior cavalry officer and seasoned combat veteran of two wars, was overzealous and inexperienced when dealing with Indians. Inadvertently he created new problems and quickly became involved in controversy with the Bureau of Indian Affairs. Confusion over policy in Indian affairs negated most of his victories over the Apache and Yavapai. As a result, the citizenry continued to lose confidence in the military and more and more chose to take matters into their own hands.

Before the close of 1867, the population of Yavapai County totaled 2,337. The most prominent occupation of the majority of Yavapai County citizens was recorded as 'miners.' Considering that the entire population of Arizona Territory that year was 7,136, it seems significant that almost 1/3 of that population was concentrated in north central Arizona.

With the war between the Indians and whites accelerating, Gen. Gregg declared all Indians in Arizona 'hostile' and revoked all passes and permits. This only made matters worse. The raids, killing and hatred on both sides increased even more. When twelve Yavapai gathered for a peace conference at La Paz on September 24, 1867, they were gunned down and all were killed.

By the summer of 1868, troops in Northern Arizona recorded 46 expeditions against the Yavapai and Apaches during that fiscal year. Despite army reports that 114 Indians had been killed, 35 wounded and many rancheras burned, Indian attacks continued to increase, and the Indians seemed to be gaining the upper hand.

On May 6, 1869, one hundred Apaches attacked a military wagon train at the foot of Grief Hill within sight of Camp Verde. It was a massacre for which the Indians claimed victory. Two days later, the Yavapai burned down a ranch owned by Abraham McKee and a Mr. Harding in Mint Valley.

The months between 1869-70 finally reached the intolerable point for the white population of north central Arizona. The low morale of the regular troops, whose numbers were dwindling and whose supplies were grossly inadequate, allowed the Indian raids to continue unabated. There was also a high level of confusion regarding Indian policy. But by the close of 1870, the army sent an increased number of troops into the territory. Thereafter, desertions decreased and the troops, under new command from Gen. O.C Ord, became better trained and more disciplined. Ord also ended confusion regarding Indian policy. His orders: "I believe the hostile Indians of Arizona should be destroyed, and I encourage troops to capture and route out Indians by every means, and hunt them down as wild animals." This became the popular 'extermination' policy regarding the 'Indian problem.'

By July of 1870, the Yavapai requested peace treaty talks with the military at Camp Date Creek, and finally Chief O-hat-che-come-e and 225 of his people succeeded in following through with this treaty. It by no means ended the Indian battles... and before long, even this chief was back on the war path.

On September 9, 1871, the Yavapai and military fought in Chino Valley resulting in death of one citizen. Before this encounter, twenty-five men of the Third cavalry with Scout Dan O'leary and his Walapai tracker leading, had lost the trail of these hostiles near Chino Valley.

Two civilians volunteered to go in search of the Yavapai if they could borrow the Walapai tracker. Later, when these same two citizens returned, they threw down a scalp and said they had run into four Indians and killed one. Eventually they admitted this was a lie. The scalp actually was that of the Walapai tracker. "What the hell," they said, "he was only an Indian."

One month later, on November 5, a stagecoach was attacked. Known as the "Wickenberg Massacre" this stagecoach, traveling with eight people on board, was attacked and six persons were killed outright. Another died later of wounds. Among those killed were three members of the George M. Wheeler surveying party. One was Frederick W. Loring of Massachusetts, a young writer widely known in the East.

Initially there was some confusion over who perpetrated the attack. At first the Prescott papers reported it was the work of Mexican bandits from Sonora. Following his investigation, Col. N.A.M. Dudley wrote the U.S. Board of Indian Commissioners that he did not believe there was an Indian in sight of the murders because Indians would have taken the blankets and horses. What was taken was a valuable shipment of gold bullion.

The sole survivor of the massacre, Molly Sheppard "a notorious courtesan from Prescott," claimed it was the work of white men. Nevertheless, it became more expedient to blame the Date Creek Indians under Chief O-hat-che-come-e, who with his followers, had bolted the reservation months earlier because of a malaria epidemic.

By August of that year, five Indians a day were dying of malaria at the Camp Date Creek reservation. Because of this, many Indians fled. Indian scouts were dispatched to track them down and kill them.

Gen. George Crook, who was called to duty in Arizona in 1871, proclaimed in General Order #10 that all roving bands of Indians were to be on reservations by Feb. 15, 1872 or be treated as hostiles.

Crook was considered one of the most successful men in dealing with the Indians that the United States ever had in its service. His

Dr. Wm. Corbusier, 1870s. Renowned Post surgeon at Fort Verde. [FVSP]

Ruins of hospital at Fort McDowell, 1990. Yavapai claim it is haunted. (photo by Kate Ruland-Thorne)

Gen. George Crook on his favorite mule ''Apache'' and accompanied by Apache scouts, tours San Carlos in the 1880s. [FVSP]

policy was "first justice, then the sword." Before his death in 1890, Crook emphatically stated that "greed and avarice on the part of the whites - in other words, the almighty dollar - was at the bottom of nine-tenths of all our Indian troubles."

From the spring of 1872 through September, the raids and killings on both sides continued at an accelerated pace. On September 1, 1872 the Indian population at Camp Date Creek doubled as a result of Crook's relentless campaign to force them back on this reservation. By September 7, Crook called for a meeting at Camp Date Creek with Chief O-hat-che-comma-e, the Yavapai leader accused of the "Wickenberg Massacre."

O-hat-che-comma-e and fifty warriors arrived for this meeting armed and painted. One of the chief's oldest enemies, Mohave Chief Irataba, pointed him out as the one responsible for the Wickenberg Massacre. When a soldier moved forward to make the arrests, one of the Yavapai pulled a knife and stabbed him. Gun fire broke out between the Yavapai and soldiers. Gen. Crook was nearly killed in the turmoil. Soldiers finally seized O-hat-che-comma-e and took him to the guardhouse.

That night, the chief attempted to escape through the guardhouse roof, but not before being pierced with a bayonet. He killed the guards, but died later in the hills north of the post. The following day, the cavalry clashed with O-hot-che-comma-e's followers near Camp Date Creek. Most of the Indians were captured and jailed.

On December 28, 1872, the "Skeleton Cave Massacre" in which 100 Yavapai men, women and children were killed during a surprise attack, finally broke the spirit of all Yavapai resistance.

Although newspapers, and army reports, described this as one of the most "terrible battles in Apache history," and reported 75 'hostiles' killed, 25 captured, the Yavapai consider it the most horrible 'massacre' in their history.

"It was in that cave that so many of our people got killed," said John Williams, a Yavapai from Fort McDowell. *"There were no Apaches there, all Yavapai. My grandfather died there. They lived in that cave and had plenty to eat. The Kakakas (mountain spirits) warned the chief in that cave to get out, but the chief wouldn't listen. He sent a boy out to bring more of our people there to come and eat with them. The soldiers got that boy and made him show them where our cave was. The next day when the people were having breakfast, the soldiers came and shot them all. The soldiers shot into that cave. The bullets hit the wall and ricocheted. All the people in that cave, men, women, children, babies got killed. Only one escaped from that cave. A girl jumped down a cliff, but broke her hip. The soldiers thought she was dead, so they left her. Later she went to Saddle Mountain where the others were. It took her two weeks to get there. No one knows how she did it. The people prayed over her and they sang over her. Later she could walk again, but not straight. She was a cripple.*

"Many sensational stories have been written about Skeleton Cave, where a band of 'bloodthirsty Apache' had been killed. These

The Gaan perform the Crown Dance at Camp Verde, 1990.
(photo by Kate Ruland-Thorne)

Members of the Fort McDowell
Indian community make 1990
pilgrimage to site of the
"Skeleton Cave Massacre."
(Louis Hood - Ft. McDowell)

Grave at Ft. McDowell containing bones of 75 Yavapai women,
men and children massacred by soldiers in 1873. (photo by Kate
Ruland-Thorne)

people who got killed were no Apache. They were Yavapai who did not want to leave their homeland and were hiding from those who wanted to chase them out. Not one soldier was killed or hurt during this event. But white people call it a 'battle'.'' (Compiled from John Williams' interview with'' James Cook of the Arizona Republic in 1970; and from THE YAVAPAI OF FORT MCDOWELL).

On April 6, 1873, Tonto Chief Cha-lipun surrendered with 2,300 men, women and children to Gen. Crook at Camp Verde.

Cha-lipun's Apache name meant "Gray Hat." He was the leader of a group who lived under the Mogollon Rim from South of Bill William's Mountain to the Young area. Also surrendering with him was Hosteen Nez, leader of a group living above the Mogollon Rim from Bill William's Mountain to the Haber area. Delshay also surrendered his group from the Tonto Basin.

"We give up," said Cha-lipun, "not because we love you (Crook), but because we are afraid of you, and because we have not only white soldiers to fight, but our own people, too." He was referring to the Indian Scout Service.

By August, Camp Date Creek was abandoned as a military post and all Indians were moved to the Rio Verde Reservation. One month later, Delshay and twelve followers fled due to another outbreak of malaria.

Delshay was a mighty outlaw warrior, although later disclaimed by both the Yavapai and Tonto Apaches. He thoroughly hated and distrusted the white man. Like Geronimo, every depredation which could in any way be linked to him, was. Delshay was a symbol of hostility and for awhile was one of the most wanted renegades in Northern Arizona.   By September 13, over 100 Indians on the Rio Verde Reservation had died of malaria, according to army reports. Yavapai historians tell another story.

They say people did die, but not from malaria. The troops, they claim, fed adults poisoned meat, and small children and babies, brown sugar laced with strychnine "which ate away their lips and gums."

On February 27, 1875, The 1500 surviving Yavapai and Tonto Apaches were removed to the San Carlos Reservation on what the Indians refer to this day - as the infamous "Trail of Tears."

"In 1873, most of the Yavapai and Tonto Apaches had been gathered in the reservation near Camp Verde. A few managed to hide out in Red Rock country around Sedona. At the reservation they were told to make irrigation ditches and start farming. There were no white man's tools for the Indians to work with. They worked with their own tools (usually sticks) and did well. But living conditions at the reservation were bad. Too many people were crowded in a small place and there was not enough food. A disease, (malaria, the whites say) killed hundreds of Yavapai. There were so many dead that the living could not gather enough wood to burn them. Despite this, the first harvest of the Yavapai turned out well. When the white settlers around the reservation saw how well these people were doing despite all their hardships, they wanted the Indians

An elderly man carries his crippled wife in a burden basket through the 180 mile journey, uncomplaining. Illustration by David Sine.

removed all together from this area. They were afraid the government would establish water rights for the Indians and give them more land. The white settlers sent delegations to Washington and told the government that the Indians on the reservation near Camp Verde all were 'Apache' and therefore should be sent to an Apache Reservation.'' (THE YAVAPAI AT FORT'' MCDOWELL)

A notorious group known as the Tucson Ring, who profited by selling inferior goods to Indian reservations, also had a hand in this removal. Only 1361 Indians would survive this "Death March" to San Carlos.

DEATH MARCH TO SAN CARLOS

"Our Indian policy, or rather the lack of a sane one, marked by broken treaties, dishonest, ignorant, and tactless handling of the entire subject and the infliction of untold misery on our Indian wards, has been such that an army man who has had to stand by with hands tied, can hardly keep within the bounds when writing or speaking about it." Brig. Gen. Wm. C. Brown. 1875.

"Somebody make bad medicine," murmured Pa-ka-ki-va, son-in-law of old war chief, Delshay. Dr. Corbusier, attending physician at the Rio Verde Indian Agency, agreed. The promises of seeds and farm equipment had been 'delayed' too many times. Corbusier also noted a strange disinterest on the part of agent Chapman toward the Indian's eagerness to plow, and enlarge the acreage that had produced such good crops the previous year. When Lt. Walter Schuyler (5th Cavalry, Company K), who was in charge of the Rio Verde reservation, received a letter from Gen. Crook, he too, became alarmed. Crook's letter had ominous overtones. It instructed Schuyler to call on Col. Brayton (Commander at Camp Verde 16 miles away) "in case of any trouble." There was no explanation as to what that" trouble might be. By now, Corbusier and Schuyler were convinced that someone indeed was 'making bad medicine'.

The chiefs of the 1,500 Tonto Apache and Yavapai people, who lived on the Rio Verde River reservation, were just as suspicious. They asked Lt. Schuyler and the doctor to find out why Indian agent Oliver Chapman was evasive when asked about the delay in the seeds and farm equipment. Why, they also asked, did issuing day come and go with only a portion of their rations being distributed? The excuse given by Chapman was "the supply train had broken down." Not a single chief believed him.

Then pandemonium erupted. Two Apache runners from the San Carlos Reservation (who had relatives at Rio Verde) sneaked into the reservation and warned the chiefs that the San Carlos Indian agent was preparing to receive more Indians. The Rio Verde Indians, who for nearly two years had been peaceful and productive, now exploded into hysteria.

Chanting and wailing filled the air. Dr. Corbusier and his wife, Fanny, were besieged with questions from the Indians who had

---

come to rely upon and trust them. Torches flickered all night in the disturbed mountain camps. When a band of Tontos, dressed in war paint, loomed before agent Chapman's tent and made threatening gestures, the agent panicked. A courier was dispatched immediately to Camp Verde. After receiving it, Gen. Crook alerted all the troops at nearby posts to prepare for possible action.

Within days, special agent Edwin Dudley arrived with his assistants and informed Indian agent Chapman that General Grant wanted all the Indian families at the Rio Verde Reservation moved to San Carlos - IMMEDIATELY!. Like a blast from a Winchester rifle, word shot through the reservation nearly causing a riot.

Small groups banded together with the intention of killing Dudley. Once again, Dr. Corbusier and his wife managed to calm the Indians. But, when Dudley ordered the chiefs to meet with him the next day, each one flatly refused. Again, Dr. Corbusier was called in to assist, much to the chagrin of Dudley.

By now, Dudley had announced his intention to move the Indians across the mountains, instead of on the roads that traversed around them. He would take them on a route across old Indian trails from Camp Verde south to East Verde, then through the valley to Rye. From there to the confluence of the Salt River and Tonto Creek, to Globe and San Carlos. Foolishly he ignored the pleas that followed.

Both Corbusier and Schuyler begged Dudley not to inflict such hardships upon these people. "It is the dead of winter," they argued. "Please, use the wagon roads around the mountains instead. Then teams can be used to transport sufficient supplies, and some of the older people and children."

Dudley vigorously shook his head - no. "Going" over the mountains is the shortest route," he shot back. "I must get them there quickly."

"But, not even beef-on-the-hoof can tolerate such rugged country, especially at this time of year," pleaded Dr. Corbusier.

"It is your duty to protect these people," shouted Schuyler - "not order them on such a difficult march!"

"I come from the highest authority in the country," Dudley bellowed. "My word is the law. Besides...they're only Indians. Let the beggars walk!"

The madness of these shocking official orders sickened and disgusted both Corbusier and Schuyler, but they knew there was nothing they could do to stop it.

Despite the tense circumstances, Dr. Corbusier dutifully circulated among the chiefs and persuaded them to meet with Dudley the next morning. Young bucks, stripped down and ready for action, joined the chiefs as they gathered in front of Dudley's tent. Nearby, Schuyler, his troop and Indian scouts watched...and pretended to be unconcerned about 600 well-armed Indians. Dr. Corbusier later recalled that cold, snowy February morning in the book, VERDE TO SAN CARLOS.

"After the chiefs had assembled, and waited about a half-an-hour, Dudley came out of his tent. He leisurely threw a buffalo robe on the step, sat down on it lopped over - resting one elbow on the robe as he talked. I stood just back of the crowd in order to listen to what might be said by the onlookers. Dudley spoke in thickened English while the interpreter translated his remarks.

"I heard a buck say in a low tone, 'He is drunk,' and turning to me, he repeated the remark. I just pointed and told him to listen."

Through an interpreter, Dudley read his orders to remove the Indians. He emphasized that they would be going to a much better place, where they could be together with their friends. Then, for no apparent reason, Dudley abruptly stood up and walked back into his tent.

"He went to get another drink, one of the chiefs murmured. This suspicion spread throughout the assembly. When Dudley returned and flopped back down on the buffalo robe, the crowd was dead silent. Two rifles clicked. Dr. Corbusier leaned against the bucks who had cocked their rifles. They let their hammers down. Dudley resumed talking, his words incoherent, even to the doctor. When Dudley finished speaking, Captain Snooks, spokesman for the chiefs, stepped forward.

"We will not go where we will be outnumbered by our enemies," he said. "Our fathers and grandfathers were born here and died here. Our wives and children were born here. The father in Washington promised that the country along the river and 10 miles on each side would be ours forever. This is little enough land for people who are accustomed to roaming for many miles before the white man came and stole our land from us."

Dudley yawned and stared blankly at the Indians. Snooks speech had not made any impression. Snooks moved closer and continued to plead. His speech was a masterpiece of oratory. He asked Dudley not to drink any more whiskey, so that he might know what he was asking of them. Other chiefs stepped forward and joined in the plea. Dudley waved them away and returned to his tent. The meeting was over.

Six days after his arrival at Rio Verde, Dudley started 1500 Indians, all on foot, across 180 miles of rough trails, over high mountains, and through numerous streams that were likely at any hour to rise many feet and become impassable. Not a single conveyance was provided to carry their extra loads.

Non-Indians who accompanied the exodus consisted of Indian agent Chapman and two assistants; Commissioner Dudley and two assistants; Chief of Scouts, Al Sieber and a small contingent of his Indian scouts; Harry Hawes, chief packer and four mule-skinners; and Lt. George Eaton commanding a troop of 15 cavalrymen. Although he was not ordered to do so, Dr. Corbusier agreed to accompany these people whom he had befriended,

Yavapai woman carrying water to her 'wikiup.' By the 1900s, canvas had replaced brush thatch. [SHM]

Yavapai women at San Carlos c. 1900. [SHM]

because a group of chiefs insisted that they needed him along. Dr. Corbusier's family watched the sad procession. . .a sight his wife would never forget:

"On February 27, 1875, the long, silent and sad procession slowly passed. They had to carry all their belongings on their backs and in their V-shaped baskets, old and young with heavy packs. One old man placed his aged and decrepit wife in one of these baskets, with her feet hanging out, and carried her on his back, the basket supported by a band over his head, almost all the way. He refused help, except at several stream crossings, where he was persuaded to allow a trooper to take her across on his horse. Over the roughest country, through thick brush and rocks - day after day, he struggled along with his precious burden - uncomplaining." (VERDE TO SAN CARLOS)

Mabel Dogka, whose parents were among the children forced into joining that cruel march, related her parent's version of the story. *"They told us this story over and over,"* said Mabel, *"so that we would never forget.*

"One day the soldiers came and told my people to move out. None of them understood English, so they don't know why they play this dirty trick on my people. The people had promised to farm if they could stay on their land. They had never been farmers before, but they were willing to do this.

"When they were moved, they had hardly any clothes and no roads to walk on. They wore moccasin shoes. Going through rocks, their shoes wear out. Some of them had to tear the blanket and wrap it around their feet. The river was really high. My people were afraid to cross it. But, the soldiers, they horse-whipped them and made them do it anyway. Since they had hardly any clothes on, they just bleed when they are whipped. Many of them died in that river. My mother (an Apache born at Indian Gardens) and father were very young at that time, but they went through it.

"My people had to carry their babies and all their belongings. Soon it was too much for them, so they had to hang their babies (who were in cradle boards) in cedar trees because they couldn't carry them any more. That's why they call it the March of Tears. My people cried all the way to San Carlos."

Dr. Corbusier reported that at least one baby was born each day on the march. "Whenever the mother felt the urge, she would go off into the bushes, unattended, and emerge later with a baby. There seldom was a blanket to wrap it in, so the babies made the trip naked, and many of them froze to death."

The medicine men, who saw evil omens at every turn, chanted and wailed, and daily reminded Dudley of the broken promises which had been made to their people. After only one week into the march, Dudley and his assistants already were sick of their jobs...in fact two of Dudley's assistants deserted, and were not seen nor heard from again.

Hunger and anger increased daily. Trying to drive cattle and foot-sore, frustrated people up steep, snow covered trails was becoming almost unbearable. When the group reached Strawberry Creek,

Lt. George O. Eaton, 5th Cavalry. [FVSP]

five miles south of the present day Childs, they found the usually quiet creek had become a raging torrent due to a huge storm the day before. Of the three crossings the Indians were forced to make, Strawberry Creek would become the most devastating. Al Sieber and Lt. Eaton urged Dudley to delay the crossing for a few days until the waters had subsided.

"You've impeded the progress of this journey long enough with your silly fears," screeched Dudley. Later, Dudley would write his official report about the crossing: "We fortunately found the 'stream' could be forded . . . sad duty to compel men, women and children, to 'wade' through cold water . . . even though they were 'Indians.' The water was about waist deep to a tall man, and the crossing was a pitiful sight."

One can only be amazed, given his attitude toward Indians, that Dudley expressed any sympathy at all in his report. But such as it was, 'pitiful' hardly seems the appropriate word . . . unconscionable would have been more fitting.

Strawberry Creek was a raging river, much higher than any 'tall man's waist,' according to Dr. Corbusier's report. Debris and rock had piled up forming dams that would suddenly break loose, furiously crashing into its human victims. Some sympathetic soldiers passed ropes to those who were less able to withstand the force of the rushing water. Others offered to carry babies, small children and the old across on their horses. Then there were those who followed Dudley's commands, and used their bull whips. For days after the crossing, Dr. Corbusier was kept busy applying splints to broken bones, and administering to the injured, sick and dying. Two more dangerous river crossings were forced upon the people. But these crossings were only a prelude to more unconscionable suffering which soon would follow.

By the second week, the beef and flour gave out, compelling the starving people to eat Canadian thistle (a poisonous plant) and the stalks of agave. There was plenty of game, according to Dr. Corbusier, but the Indians were not 'allowed' to hunt. One night when a confused deer wandered in above their camp, Al Seiber shot it. Then the Yavapais from above the camp and the Tontos camped below, descended on the carcass. There was a frenzied melee which ended in the Tontos emerging with the prize, driving all others away.

Author's Note: *One wonders how a troop of 15 cavalrymen and a handful of scouts managed to keep 1500 starving Indians from hunting? Could it be that all weaponry was removed from the possession of the Indians prior to the march? Perhaps that might explain why unarmed Indians tolerated 'orders not to hunt' even though they were starving . . . they had no choice. It also might explain why these tormented people continued to remain on such a hideous march while under the guard of such a small contingent of well-armed soldiers and scouts. Members of the Yavapai tribe at Ft. McDowell informed this writer in July 1990, that*

"Broken Arrow" - a classic movie filmed in Sedona in the 1950s starred Jeff Chandler (standing back) as Cochise and Debra Pagent (end left) as Apache love interest for James Stewart. Mabel Dogka (middle foreground) was one of the 'extras' in the movie. (courtesy of Mabel Dogka)

Mabel Dogka - Oldest living member of the Yavapai-Apache people of Camp Verde and Clarkdale, 1990. (photo by Kate Ruland-Thorne)

not only were all rifles removed from the Indians before the march, but all knives and anything else that might be considered a weapon. This information will not be found in any official army reports. ***

Old feuds between the Yavapai and Tonto Apaches were soon rekindled, and spasmodic war dances began. (Their feuding originally began when the Yavapai joined the ranks as Scouts during their Date Creek Reservation years, and helped track the Tontos, whom they blamed for all their troubles.)

For the first time, Dudley realized he had reason to fear for his life. On March 8, twelve days into the march, all hell broke loose. Dr. Corbusier recorded the events as he remembered them: *"Just after we made camp on the East branch of the Verde River (near Bloody Basin), the Western and Eastern Yavapais came in fighting-hungry and in an ugly frame of mind. Their women began to shout, "Kill the Tontos." Shortly, fifty naked warriors charged passed us. Dudley, Agent Chapman and their men tried to drive them back by waving their arms and shouting, but to no avail. The Yavapais ran up a 20 foot bank of a mesa on which the Tontos were camped - dropped to their knees and began shooting. Dudley called Lt. Eaton, who with his men stood waiting authority to interfere. As the troops ran passed Dudley, Chapman and their assistants, the soldiers noticed them on their knees, under a tree - praying. The troopers then drove the Indians down the hill."* (VERDE TO SAN CARLOS)"

Author Dan L. Thrapp, in his book AL SIEBER - CHIEF OF SCOUTS, (University of Oklahoma Press), researched Lt. Eaton's account of this event, a manuscript written 50 years after his involvement, and found many discrepancies in his report. According to Eaton's report, *"a fight broke out between two Indian camps. He (Eaton) and his troops stood their ground between the warring factions - he with his hands upraised - and through an interpreter, called the three leading chiefs together and 'bawled them out.' After some difficulty,"* he said, *"he was able to call the fight off."*

Author Thrapp claims it was Al Seiber who actually stood amidst a "hail of bullets and cowed them (the Indians) into ceasing fire without he himself firing a shot."

Commissioner Dudley's report of the incident supports Thrapp's claim: *"A difficulty occurred,"* wrote Dudley, *"which resulted in a general fight between the two tribes...The escort under direction of Mr. Al Sieber, Chief of General Crook's scouts, at once took a position between two contending parties and made every effort to send them to their respective camps, and success attended their efforts. When the loss came to be counted, we knew of five dead, the Indians said seven, and ten wounded. Not a great loss when so much lead was expended."*

Dr. Corbusier stated that after the 'fight', he climbed to the top of the mesa and found 25 Indians sprawled out in various positions (he doesn't say whether they were wounded - or dead) and treated the 10 worst wounded. "Estimates of the dead varied up to 30," he wrote, "but I found four." (VERDE TO SAN CARLOS). Both sides do agree that none of the whites were shot.

Mabel Dogka claims there never was a 'fight' - only a massacre:

"When you drive to Phoenix, you see a sign that says 'Bloody Basin.' That's my people's blood. That was when they said, no, we won't go any further, so the soldiers opened fire on them and their blood just flowed like a river. The same way with Skull Valley, it was full of Indian heads. White man say that is where Indians kill white people. That makes me mad. I want to stand up and shout, you're wrong. It was a place where white people killed many of my people. They say it the other way because they want their side to look good. Same way with making my people cross the rivers. They don't tell how the soldiers whipped them with bull whips to make them cross those rivers. There was not a wagon any where on that trip to help carry my people, who were too old, or young, or sick to walk."

David Sine, Yavapai-Apache, said that if a fight did erupt, there were certainly no guns, so it was probably a free-for-all. Also, he states, there was no division between the tribes at this time. The Tonto and Yavapai were all one. It is likely, he contends, that the soldiers simply took the 'troublemakers' to the top of the hill and shot them, along with anyone who was too sick or weak to continue the journey.

Dr. Corbusier reported that the ten wounded Indians were either slung over the shoulders of some younger Indians, or carried in a crude litter attended by the medicine men, whose piercing chants echoed for days throughout the Mazatzal Wilderness.

The third cruel river crossing lay ahead (the Salt River) before they faced the grueling climb up the steep Apache Trail near the present Roosevelt Dam. The old and the crippled finally sat down on the trail, unable to move another step. Soon, they were whipped to their feet. The trail was so narrow that horses had to be led. A few of the troopers carried screaming, terrified children, who clung to them desperately. Suddenly a mule lost its footing and plunged into the river far below, carrying with it what was left of the much needed supplies.

By the next day, the Yavapai men had painted their faces for war. Beneath the paint were penetrating looks of hatred. Dudley lost no time in leaving his charges on the pretense of going ahead to San Carlos to bring back food and fresh supplies.

Although Dr. Corbusier claims Dudley did meet them at their next camp with these supplies, there is no official report of his doing so. What is recorded, is that the San Carlos Indian agent Clum, accompanied by Dudley - and very likely a contingent of troops - met them at their next camp, and "escorted" the Indians the rest of the way to San Carlos.

The Yavapai claim that "food was brought to the camp. The people were so hungry, they cooked and ate it right away. The food was poisoned and many died. The ones who only held it in their hands and refused to eat it (remembering past experiences), just got sick."

Of the 1500 Indians who left the Rio Verde Reservation six weeks before, various estimates indicate that approximately 375 either escaped, or did not survive the journey. These estimates do not include the numerous babies who were born, and died along the way.

The March of Tears was the last act in Dudley's government career. He stated in his final report that the move was a difficult one, but successfully made. When he turned in his expense account, he found himself gypped out of all money. In his protest to Commissioner Edward Smith he wrote: *"Myself, the Indians, the employees who were with me, the military escort, the pack train - all took their lives in their hands and knew that at any time they might be in danger of losing their lives. And you sit in a nicely carpeted office and forget more in one day about this miserable place than those of us who came over it ever knew. I am aggrieved that you should fail to give me the small amount of money that was necessary."*

On his way back to San Carlos, Dr. Corbusier disinterred several heads of Indians killed at Bloody Basin and sent them to a medical museum. The skulls showed the so-called explosive action passing through the skull, (gatling guns?) which broke it into many pieces. (De Coursey 1951: Letter). This seemed a curious thing for the doctor to have done.

Following the March of Tears, and the closing of the Rio Verde Agency, Corbusier continued to serve as Post Surgeon for the army at 15 other Indian agencies throughout the country.

During the expedition to the Philippines in 1898, he organized the Red Cross Society and initiated the first "dog tags" issued to soldiers. He also organized and trained the first female nurses to serve in the United States Army. He retired from active service with the rank of Lt. Col. in 1908 at the age of 64, only to be recalled again at the outbreak of World War I to serve in Court-Martial duty. Dr. William Henry Corbusier was finally relieved from active duty in 1919, following a distinguished and humanitarian career.

Agent John Philip Clum who took charge of the Indians at San Carlos was only 23 years old at the time. Although a "greenhorn" when it came handling Indians, he nevertheless was one of the few Indian agents who tried to be honest.

Nominated by the Dutch Reform Church to the federal government post at San Carlos, he promptly made himself "boss" of the Apaches and severed all relations with the Interior Department. Against army regulations, Clum organized the first Apache police force and Apache Court. When Geronimo bolted the reservation in 1877, Clum and 40 members of his force, walked all the way to Santa Fe and arrested 17 renegades, including Geronimo.

By 1877, however, Clum left the service in a huff, frustrated by the constant obstacles put in his path. He would go on to found Tombstone's famous EPITAPH newspaper, as well as become the town's mayor and postmaster. Unfortunately for the Indian people at San Carlos, one of the most corrupt Indian Agents ever to hold that position, would take his place - J.C. Tiffany.

SAN CARLOS TO THE PRESENT

The various bands of Apache and Yavapai people who were finally gathered together at San Carlos in 1875, did not constitute a united people. Separated by the Gila River, the Yavapai lived south in an area called the Mineral Strip, and the Tontos were located to the north. But separation did not prevent the suspicion and hostility which raged between them. The only thing anyone agreed upon was their hereditary hatred for the white man, and their unified dislike for the hot, unhealthful San Carlos Reservation. Every Indian there longed to return to his ancestral land.

By 1882, the Indians at San Carlos had been treated so outrageously by Agent J.C. Tiffany that many were once again on the war path. One major outbreak resulted in the Battle of Big Dry Wash in the Verde Valley following "The Cibicue Massacre." On September 4, 1882, General George Crook was recalled to command the Department of Arizona.

When Crook arrived at San Carlos, he found out just how badly things had gone during his absence. Crook protested vehemently against the government policy of forcing these people together initially. No one had listened. Now he saw first hand the consequences of this policy, and the monumental task that lay before him.

On his mule, Apache, Crook rode throughout the reservation and listened to each grievance. Immediately he expelled from the reservation all squatters, miners and friends of the Indian agent who had been plundering the Indians and the government for years.

The second month after Crook's arrival, a Federal Grand Jury concluded that, *"for several years, the people of the Territory have been gradually arriving at the conclusion that the management of the Indian reservations in Arizona has been a fraud upon the government; that the constantly reoccurring outbreaks of the Indians and their consequent devastations were due to criminal neglect or apathy of the Indian agent at San Carlos; but never until the present investigations of the Grand Jury have laid bare the infamy of Agent Tiffany could a proper idea be formed of the fraud and villainy which were constantly practiced in open violation of the law. . . and in defiance of public justice. . .and is a disgrace to the civilization of the age and a foul blot upon the national escutcheon. . ."* Washington relieved Tiffany of his office, but the damage had already been done.

Geronimo and Nachez and 120 men, women and children soon bolted the reservation again and dealt death and destruction everywhere they went. The Yavapai and Tonto Apaches, both men and women, volunteered as Scouts after Crook promised that all Indians who helped catch Geronimo, could go back to their homeland. Three years after the campaign began, Geronimo, Nachez and their band were rounded up on September 8, 1886 and put on a train for Florida. A Camp Verde Scout by the name of

Captain Smiley was instrumental in Geronimo's final capture.

By the following year, the settlers in the Verde Valley were alarmed to learn that the Yavapai and Apache had been given permission to return to their homeland because of their outstanding service for the government. Immediately political pressure was applied to stop their return. A letter writing campaign was initiated by the Valley's prominent citizens to the 7th Territorial Governor, C.M. Zulick:

Sir:

The undersigned citizens of the Verde Valley and vicinity wish to enter a protest against the settlement of Indians upon the Camp Verde Military reservation.

The actual settlers here who have acquired title to the government land feel that it would be an act of injustice to destroy the prospect of making future homes here by having a band of uncivilized Indians moving in our midst.

That whereas now peace and order are the rule, with the addition of Indians, all sense of security would be gone.

The Indians themselves would destroy confidence in the community, and added to them would be the camp followers who are less desirable than the Indians.

Homes are being built up here and improvements made with the expectation that we were forever free from Indian intrusion. With their coming, all progress and social prospects cease.

The fact that there are 300 families settled along the narrow valley, all prosperous, who shudder for what the future might bring if they are driven out by having a band of lawless Indians forced upon them as neighbors.

We hope that you will represent our case to the authorities in Washington and show our many good reasons for objecting to their transfer to this valley.

> *Respectfully,*
> *W.G. Wingfield,*
> *J.B. Ricketts,*
> *and J.G. Crum - farmers.*

The Yavapai and Apaches were not allowed to return, but in 1900, they simply walked away from San Carlos - wisely not bothering to ask permission. When the Wipukapayas and Dil'zeae arrived in their beloved valley, they discovered the best land had been taken over by white settlers. Mabel Dogka picks up the story:

"My people left San Carlos. . .even the mineral strip that was given to them and the cattle. They don't want any of it. They just walked away and came back to the Verde Valley where they had lived and roamed for all time. When they came back, they found there is a mine going on (Jerome), and they know why they were sent away in the first place. My mother and father came back with their people." Mabel's father, who had been a member of Agent Clum's celebrated Apache Police (called "Catch Thems") later took the surname of Kitchiyan, which means Catch Them.

"My mother would go to white houses and make a gesture of

Each year, Yavapai
and Apache people
gather at Camp Verde
on February 24 to
commemorate those
who suffered and died
on the terrible "Death
March to San Carlos"
in 1875. (photo by Kate
Ruland-Thorne)

"WE ARE YAVAPAI" -
Today, the People of
the Sun are trying to
re-establish their iden-
tity, which they feel
was taken from them
along with their lands
when early white set-
tlers and miners mis-
took them for Apaches
in the 1860s.

Modern day 'social dance' at
Camp Verde, 1990. (photo by
Kate Ruland-Thorne

Miss Yavapai-Apache, 1990,
Lisa Jackson, talented young
Yavapai woman, and
honor student at N.A.U.

washing clothes, to let them know she wanted to earn money washing their clothes. My father chopped wood for the white people. We lived in a teepee house (wickiup). Some of my people squatted on company land which belonged to the United Verde. The company let them do this if they worked in the mine.

"My family lived close to where the smelter was to be built (Clarkdale). When they were ready to build the smelter, we were told to move. There was a white man who had an orchard near there. He told us not to move, but we were afraid that if we didn't move, they would send us back to San Carlos.

"There were three or four families who had to move. The white man's name was Walter Jordan. He was a nice man and good to the Indians. Jordan let the Indians gather apples. The Indians put the apples into barrels and let them ferment. They added malt and mixed it with sugar. Pretty soon, the Indians would be hollering and screaming all over the place. Jordan let them do that.

"Jordan was the one who Christianized the Indians. They don't know what a church was then. He (Jordan) was a real Christian. He gave my people vegetables, watermelons and things and paid them to pick for him.

"It makes me sad that my people have let their traditions go." (The Apaches on the other hand have retained their traditions.) "It is not good for their future. There are benefits through the tribe now, for students who graduate from high school. Everyone who does, can get a $5,000 scholarship to college. This is good."

Today, remnants of the once proud and prosperous People of the Sun and Dil'zeae move into the 21st Century with determination, purpose and the hope for long-range financial independence. The Tolkepaya, or Western Yavapai, whose boundaries once extended from the Bradshaw Mountains to Yuma are now known as the "Yavapai-Prescott Tribe, and have 115 registered Yavapai on their reservation." In 1935, 75 acres of land was transferred to them from the old Fort Whipple Military Reserve. This created the only reserve just for Yavapai Indians.

In establishing the reservation, the government also issued two cows to each family as a potential source of income. Over the years, the increasing size of this herd led to the government's decision to add 1,320 acres, also on the military reserve, to the Yavapai-Prescott Reservation.

With the establishment of the reservation, Sam Jimulla (Gee-mu-la) was appointed Chief of the Prescott Yavapais by the Commissioner of Indian Affairs, and simultaneously elected as Chief by his own people. He was succeeded by his wife, Viola following his death in 1940. A devout Christian, Viola organized the first Indian Presbyterian Mission and was known for her talent as a basket weaver. At the time of her appointment, she was the only woman Chief among American Indians. After her death in 1966 at the age of 88, Viola was inducted into the Arizona Women's Hall of Fame.

In the 55 years since they became an official reservation, the

Violet Jimulla - First woman "chief" in America and leader of the Yavapai-Prescott tribe. [SHM]

Women of the Yavapai-Prescott tribe revive their ancient art of basket-weaving. 1940s. [SHM]

Tolkepaya, or Prescott Yavapaies have set aside portions of their
small reservation for The Sun Dog Industrial Park on Highway
89, one of their first ventures, and the Sheraton Resort and Conference Center which opened in 1988 through the efforts of
developer Bill Grace. The tribe is now working with Grace to
develop a 30-acre shopping center fronting Highway 69 to be
anchored by Wall Mart. In addition, the tribe's bingo and Smoke
Shops were relocated on Hwy. 69 near the Sheraton Resort and
planned shopping center. Presently the tribe is working with the
city of Prescott to provide educational resources for their youth,
and are striving to revive and preserve the rich heritage of their
culture.

The Kwevikopaya, or Southeastern Yavapai who lived in the
Mazatzal-Four Peak and Superstition Mountain region were granted
a 24,689 acre reservation in 1903 at the old Fort McDowell Military
Reserve. This is the largest of the Yavapai and Apache's three reservations in terms of acreage and it is certainly the most valuable.

Located at the confluence of the Salt and Verde Rivers, the Fort
McDowell "Mohave-Apache" reservation is situated in the heart
of two of Arizona's most expensive developments - Scottsdale and
Fountain Hills. Since 1910, members of this tribe have had an on-
going, non-stop battle to retain this valuable piece of real estate,
and their invaluable water rights to the Verde River.

The 1910 Kent Decree stipulated that the Fort McDowell residents
should be moved to the Salt River Pima Reservation, where their
water rights would have been reduced considerably. For over 25
years, the tribe continually blocked these relocation efforts. Dr.
Carlos Montezuma, a Yavapai captured as a boy by the Pimas, sold
into white society and educated as one of the first American
Indian medical doctors, was instrumental in blocking the relocation efforts and saving the reservation for his people. In 1923,
Montezuma, who became one of the most famous Indians in the
United States from 1890 until his death, chose to die among his
people in a wikiup on the Verde River at Fort McDowell in 1923.
It was Montezuma who initiated the drive to give Native Americans
the right to vote, and one year after his death, in 1924, this long
over due privilege was finally granted.

Presently the Fort McDowell tribe (whose enrollment is 688
Yavapai and Apache), is fighting government attempts to build the
Orm Dam, a component of the Central Arizona Project, which
would cover most of the reservation at Fort McDowell with water.
Such a dam would provide water considered 'essential' for the
swimming pools and golf courses of their wealthy nearby neighbors.
The "Indian Wars" are not over yet. They just take place in court-
rooms now, instead of mountains, and water has replaced gold as
the source of contention.

The Wipukapaya, people of the red rocks, and the Dil'zeae whose
land once ranged from Bill Williams Mountain to Granite Peak

"Wassaja" with Carlos Gentile. Gentile bought Wassaja for $30. This five year old Yavapai child, who was captured in a Pima raid in 1872, was renamed Carlos Montezuma, educated in the east and became one of the first American Indian medical doctors. After a visit to his people at Fort McDowell in the 1900's, he helped save them from being relocated to the Pima's Salt River Reservation. He also was instrumental in getting American Indians the right to vote in 1924 and was one of the most famous Native Americans in the country from 1900 until his death in 1923. Arizona State University - Heyden Collection.

Grave of Carlos Montezuma at Fort McDowell. When Dr. Montezuma realized he was dying of tuberculosis, he returned to his people at Fort McDowell, shed all white trappings and stayed in a wikiup near the Verde River where he later died. Members of his family insisted on taking care of him despite his warnings against it, and all died of tuberculosis as well. (photo by Kate Ruland-Thorne)

near Prescott, (the Dil'zeae roamed from Bill Williams Mountain to Show Low and Young and throughout the Tonto Basin) returned to the Camp Verde area in 1898 with nothing but hope that land would still be available. What they found was only a future of hard labor and sacrifice. Things have never been easy for them, even to this day. "Our neighboring communities still do not understand why we are here," said David Sine, a respected member of this tribe. "They only see us a people who stand in the way of their progress."

Today, the 1,092 Yavapai-Apache at Camp Verde hold 653 acres of land which includes a 150 acre farming cooperative in Middle Verde on land sold to them by the Wingfield family. North of the town of Camp Verde near where old Fort Verde is located, the tribe has built the Yavapai-Apache Visitor's Center and Cliff Castle Lodge in order to serve the thousands of annual tourists who visit their 'place of the origin,' Montezuma Well, as well as Montezuma Castle and the Tuzigoot ruins. Their land holdings were recently increased by 54.4 acres when the Phelps-Dodge Corporation granted land to its Indian employees at their copper mine outside of Clarkdale in 1969.

All three groups are striving for self-determination and self-government, education for their children, and an ability to stand proudly alongside all of their American neighbors.

In the 1960's, the Tonto and Yavapai tribes united to make claims against the U.S. Government for the lands taken from them in the 1860s. A court settlement awarded them fifty cents per acre for the 10 million acres that had once been their home.

It does seem ironic, however, that each of these small Yavapai and/or Apache reservations now provide a refuge for them on or near the very forts which were historically established to exterminate them as a people.

Looking to the future, which is in the hands of the young.
(photo by Kate Ruland-Thorne)

GENERAL GEORGE CROOK (1829 - 1890)

General George Crook was known to the Indians as Nan-Tan-Lupan (Chief Grey Wolf). His attitude toward the Indians was different from that of his predecessors. He had a better understanding of the Indian's problems, and more compassion toward their plight, even though many of the present-day Apaches and Yavapai may not agree with that assumption.

As to General Crook's appearance, a description by Captain John Bourke, who served under him, details it best:

"His personal appearance was impressive, but without the slightest suggestion of the pompous and overdressed military man; he was as plain as an old stick, and looked more like an honest country squire than the commander of a war-like expedition. He had blue-grey eyes, quick and penetrating in his glance, a finely chiseled Roman nose, a firm and yet kindly mouth, a well-arched head, a good brow and a general expression of indomitable resolution, honest purpose, sagacity, and good intentions. He had an aversion to wearing a uniform, and to the glitter and filigree of the military profession. He was essentially a man of action, and spoke but little, and to the point, but was fond of listening to conversations of others. He was at all times accessible to the humblest soldier or the poorest "prospector," without ever losing a certain dignity which repelled familiarity, but had no semblance of haughtiness. He never used profanity and indulged in no equivocal language."

His chosen mode of transportation was his favorite mule, Apache. Capt. Bourke also noted: "Crook's council of war differed from those of any general he had known. He never asked anyone for an opinion, and never gave one of his own."

General Crook graduated from West Point in 1852, and in 1862, was wounded during the Civil War. He retained the rank of Major General before the conflict between the states ended.

Following the Civil War, Crook continued his army career, this time as an Indian fighter. Although Crook has gone down in history as one of this country's greatest Indian fighters, there are some historians who believe General Crook was too timid, slow, cautious, and at times failed to press attacks even when he had superior forces.

One interesting example was the criticism he received for his action (or non-action) when in command of a large force driving up from Fort Fetterman to protect the southern flank during the June, 1876 drive to the Little Big Horn.

General Terry and General Gibbons coming down from the north and from the east with their contingents of infantry and cavalry, were to meet with Lt. Col. George Armstrong Custer and his 7th Cavalry at Little Big Horn on June 26, 1876. Their purpose was to surround and drive renegade Indians back to the Rosebud Reservation.

Coming up from the south, Gen. Crook encountered a large band of these Indians, painted for war at the Rosebud, and a battle ensued. Although greatly outnumbering the hostiles, Crook failed

Soldiers at Fort Verde at camp during a "long" scout." 1870s. [FVSP]

A typical young Fort Verde soldier in winter dress - 1870s. (Fort Verde State Park [FVSP]

FORTS WITHOUT WALLS *Fort Whipple was typical of forts established in Arizona and the Southwest during the Indian wars from 1860s - 80s. Apaches and other 'hostile' tribes rarely if ever attacked entire forts, preferring instead to employ guerrilla tactics (fighting in small groups acting independently). It was common, however, for them to initiate early morning raids on livestock at these forts. (Sharlot Hall Museum [SHM])*

to press his advantage and instead proceeded an orderly retreat. He reasoned that his line of communication might become over extended. He also believed he had suppressed an Indian attack, a victory of its own.

The Indians, on the other hand, saw this as their victory. They believed they had turned away a large army contingent and went wild with excitement. If General Crook had pressed forward and taken the field, demoralizing this marauding group of hostiles, Custer's defeat at Little Big Horn several days later, might not have taken place.

As it was, the Indians returned to their encampment filled with 'war power' which incited the 4,000 other renegade warriors to stay their ground. Custer never knew his southern flank no longer existed, and his fate was sealed. Discovered by the Indians on June 25, a day before his reinforcements were to arrive, Custer was forced into an unexpected battle with the Indians, who outnumbered him tremendously, and the rest is history.

Prior to this infamous event, Crook had already made a name for himself in the Southwest, where his final victory over Geronimo was the climax of his military life. Crook was known for his skill as a leader against tribes, and was respected by the Indians for his honesty in dealing with them. All in all these factors helped shorten the Apache Wars and in some people's opinion, benefited both whites and Indians in the long run.

Gen. Crook had his base of command at Fort Whipple, Prescott, where he laid down his policy toward the Indians in his General Order:

"The Commanding General, after making a thorough and exhaustive examination among the Indians. . . regrets to say that he finds among them a general feeling of distrust and want of confidence in the whites, especially the soldiers; and also that much dissatisfaction, dangerous to the peace of the country, exists among them. Officers and soldiers. . .are reminded that one of the fundamental principles of the military character is justice to all - Indians as well as white man - and that a disregard of this principal is likely to bring about hostilities, and cause the deaths of the very people they are sent here to protect. In all their dealings with the Indians, officers must be careful not only to observe the strictest fidelity, but to make no promise, not in their power to carry out; all grieving arising in their jurisdiction should be redressed, so then an accumulation of them may not cause an outbreak."

Gen. Crook next ordered all squatters and unauthorized miners to remove themselves from the Camp Date Creek and Camp Verde Reservations. He even started an investigation which resulted in the reorganization of the Indian Department, and the discharge of some agents and higher-up officials in the same department.

Next, he established a military trail, which today is known as General Crook's Trail. This trail began at Fort Whipple in Prescott, and ended at Fort Apache. Both of these forts, and the Crook

YAVAPAI SCOUTS - 1870s. Chief of Scouts Al Sieber preferred the Tonto Apache scouts over Yavapai because the Yavapai insisted on four days of a purification ceremony following each scouting expedition, particularly if any killing was involved. Tontos did not adhere to such requirements, and therefore did not slow expeditions down. [SHM]

Capt. J.C. Burke, Capt. McGonigle and General George Crook. 1880s. [SHM]

Trail, are still in existence. The 175 mile-long trail traverses the Verde Valley, cuts through the pine wilderness of the higher terrain of the Mogollon Rim, and ends at Fort Apache in the White Mountains.

In her delightful book, VANISHING ARIZONA, Martha Summmerhayes recalled her own excursion along the Crook Trail in the 1870s. She relates her experience as a young Army wife, accompanying her Lieutenant husband to Fort Apache. She was the first woman to travel by wagon along Crook's Trail.

Camping along the trail at night, Martha could not free herself from anxiety of an Apache attack. Everywhere she looked, she imagined a fierce Apache behind a dark tree trunk. Seeking assurance one night from her husband, he patted her lovingly and told her she could feel safe about going to sleep. "The Apaches never attack at night," he said. Several minutes later, Martha whispered. . ."When do they attack?". . ."Just before dawn," he yawned.

Unbeknownst to Martha Summerhayes, she had as much reason to fear the Yavapai warriors as she did the Apache. By the 1870s, both of these distinctly different tribes had joined forces to fight for their sacred lands in the Verde Valley. Yavapais are not Apaches, but even Crook did not bother to make this tribal distinction. This error on his part, and that of other white Americans, caused untold hardship and suffering for this Yuman-speaking tribe, who initially tried in vain to avoid war with the U.S. Army.

The major reason for Crook's eventual success in the "Apache Wars" was his establishment of the Indian Scout Service. Crook used one Indian band against another, relying on the traditional enmities that often existed between them. In his war against the Tonto Apaches and Yavapais for instance, Crook employed Scouts from the White Mountain band, whose historic association with their northern brethren rarely had been friendly. The man Crook chose most often to lead these Scouts was Chief of Scouts, Al Sieber.

INDIAN SCOUTS VERSUS INDIAN OUTLAWS

General George Crook proved that Indian Scouts were necessary in the successful elimination of Indian hostiles in Northern Arizona. The main figures in that triumph were the civilian and army leaders who controlled, managed, led and inspired those Indian Scouts. They were known as Chief of Scouts. Normally they were not the officers in command, but as head of all Scouts, they were actually in command in the truest sense of the word. Commanding officers learned quickly while in the field to base their decisions upon whatever their Chief of Scouts advised. Such were the likes of Al Sieber, Tom Horn, Dan O'Leary and Mickey Free, and others, all well-known Chief of Scouts in the Verde Valley.

Mickey Free had been captured by the Apaches when he was a boy, and had not been treated well by them. As a Scout, he

Mickey Free, one of the least trusted and least liked scouts among the Indians he led. [FVSP]

Al Sieber, Chief of Scouts, 1870s. [FVSP]

Tonto Apache scouts at Fort Verde, 1870-80s. [FVSP]

Al Sieber (middle) with Tonto scouts, 1870s. [FVSP]

delighted in their suffering, and took great satisfaction in helping to exterminate them whenever possible. Of all the Scouts, he was the least liked and respected by Indian people. Al Sieber, who worked with Mickey Free, once described him as "half" Mexican, half Irish and whole son-of-a-bitch."

Cochise, the famous leader of the Chiruachua Apaches, was wrongly accused of Free's childhood kidnaping in 1860. It was because of this, and the unbelievable bungling by a greenhorn lieutenant, that one of the most vicious Apache uprisings in the Southwest erupted.

In 1861, Cochise was accused of stealing Mickey Free from a ranch near Fort Buchanan. Like most Apaches, Cochise had a bitter hatred and distrust for all white men, which stemmed from an incident in which his wife and children were slaughtered.

But Cochise had been at peace for awhile when the 7th Cavalry camped near his stronghold on Apache Pass. One Lieut. George Bascom was sent to retrieve the child, Mickey Free, from Cochise' encampment. Cochise, along with some warriors, came to Bascom's tent to talk to him. As soon as Cochise arrived, the soldiers tried to take him into custody. Cochise drew a knife and slashed his way out of the tent, leaving his fellow warriors to be seized as hostages. Cochise immediately captured several white men to assure an exchange of prisoners. Due to Bascom's bungling, the exchange never took place. Furious, Cochise saw to it that the white men were tortured and put to death. The soldiers retaliated by hanging the Indians, and a vicious war began again.

During this war of hatred, it is a known historical fact that Cochise tortured at least 16 prisoners by dragging them behind horses with a rope until they died. He was known to have burned 18 men alive at the stake, and tortured many others by cutting flesh slowly from their bodies until they died in agonizing, screaming pain. With this kind of statistic, one can only believe Cochise was a murderous, sadistic outlaw, and truly an uncivilized savage by white man's standards. Despite Hollywood movies to the contrary, he was never of the same mold as Chief Joseph of the Nez Pearce or Crazy Horse and other respected warriors.

But, there were those who viewed him differently. One doctor, A.N. Ellis, observed Cochise during a peace conference with Gen. Granger in 1871.

"While he was talking, we had a fine opportunity to study this most remarkable man. Evidently he was about 58 years old, 5'8" tall, in person lithe and wiry, every muscle being well-rounded and firm. A silver thread was now and then visible in his otherwise black hair which he wore cut straight around his head, about level with his chin. His countenance displayed great force.

"General Granger expressed the White Father's" desire for peace. He reiterated that the land, mountains and valleys he was now in, would be part of his reservation. Cochise, expressing his doubt,

gave his speech - a sad speech, relating the unsolvable problems revolving around the white man's intrusion of his sacred homeland.

Cochise stated ...'when I was young, I walked all over the country, east and west, and saw no other people than the Apaches. After many summers, I walked again and found another race of people who had come to take it. How is it? Why is it that the Apaches want to die - that they carry their lives on their fingernails? They roam over the hills and plains, and want the heavens to fall on them. The Apaches were once a great nation; they are now but a few...many have been killed in battle...tell me, if the Virgin Mary has walked throughout all the land, why has she never entered the land of the Apache?'

Cochise ended this oratory stating he would never consent to life on the Tularosa Reservation in New Mexico. "That is a long way off," he stated. "The flies in those mountains eat out the eyes of the horses. The bad spirits live there. I have drunk of these waters...I do not want to leave here."

In spite of General Granger's promise that he would not be sent to the Tularosa Reservation, within months, that is exactly where Cochise and his people were ordered to go. Cochise kept his promise. He fled into his beloved mountains. Once again, the Apaches were on the warpath. Some 56 raids were made in the year that followed. Over 45 white people lost their lives as a result, and the numbers of wounded and amount of livestock stolen, soared.

The white man's inability to follow through on his promises, always reaped death and destruction. For the Tonto and Yavapai people of Central Arizona, however, such men as Crook and Al Sieber went out of their way to be honest and straight forward in their dealings with the Indians. After Crook took control in Central and Northern Arizona in 1871, the Indian Wars came to a speedy conclusion, simply because men like Crook and Al Sieber kept their word.

Al Sieber was not only honest in his dealings with the Indians, he was considered a gentleman among his own people. Tom Horn, another respected Chief of Scouts, and Al Sieber were great friends and shared many adventures together. Like Sieber, Horn was known as an excellent Chief of Scouts. Unfortunately, Horn was hanged in Montana many years after the Indian Wars, for a crime he did not commit.

In the final containment of the Southwest, the value of Crook's Indian Scouts proved a case in point. During the period between 1872-74, fewer than 20 hostile Indians were killed or captured by the regular army without using Scouts. Whereas the army units who took advantage of the Indian Scout system, killed 275 hostiles and captured more than 330 during that same period. Needless to say, the value of the Scouts during the Indian Wars of Arizona Territory, was invaluable.

The way that General Crook persuaded Indians to become Scouts against their own people was by telling them: "I expect good men

---

67

to help me to run down bad ones. This is the way white people do it; if there are bad men in neighborhoods, all law-abiding citizens turn out to assist the officers of the law in arresting and punishing those who will not behave themselves. I hope that you will see it's your duty to do the same."

Being fed and clothed and put on the payroll of the U.S. Army, helped persuade many to join up. Scouting was an easy thing to do, particularly when tracking old tribal rivals. They had been doing this for centuries.

Crook used as an example to them, that the white man had outlaws too. Men like Frank and Jesse James, the Dalton Gang and Cole Younger were bad men who needed to be hunted down, just as Indian outlaws like Geronimo, Cochise and Delshay.

Not all Indian Scouts were Apaches in Arizona. To fill out the ranks, General Crook enlisted Yavapais, Walapais, Pimas and Piutes, among others. Both Crook and Sieber preferred the Tonto Apaches overall, and considered them the best Scouts. Yavapais were excellent Scouts also, but they required a four day purification ceremony following an engagement in which there was killing, and this simply slowed things down too much.

Men like Al Sieber were put in control of one Company of Indian Scouts, usually consisting of 26 Indians, who were attached to a column of cavalry. Sieber became one of Gen. Crook's most renowned Chief of Scouts.

Al Sieber was born in Rhineland, Germany in 1844. His widowed mother brought her family to America when Al was still a boy.

As an adult, Sieber stood six feet in height, and was a man of strength, and powerfully built. He had penetrating blue eyes, and wore his blond hair short. He always sported a mustache, which was common during this period.

An excellent shot, Sieber never hesitated to take aim and kill when the need arose. He maintained a loyalty among his Scouts both through fear and honest dealings. He said, "I do not deceive them, but always tell them the truth. When I say I'm going to kill them, I do it, and when I tell them I'm their friend, they know it." There was rarely a deserter among Sieber's Company of Indian Scouts.

Sieber arrived in Central Arizona during the height of the gold rush in the late 1860s. This was also the time of the Yavapai and Apache Wars in that area.

Violence raged on both sides as Arizona soil became drenched with the blood of men, women and children, both red and white. To pluck a gold nugget out of the soil, one had better be prepared to fight for it. Of course the "ignorant" Indians never understood why they had to give up their hunting grounds and way of life to satisfy the white man's lust for gold.

When Sieber arrived in Prescott in 1867, it was an established gold camp with a population of around 500. He arrived after mustering out of the Civil War, working his way westward doing odd jobs. Just 25 years of age, and without funds, he signed on to ride guard for Teamster Dan Hazzard. It was a dangerous job to bring freight into Prescott through hostile territory. From behind any bush or rock, there was a constant threat of being attacked by either marauding Indians, Mexican bandits, or plain-old outlaws.

Soon Sieber made friends with such Indian fighters as Dan O'Leary, John Townsend and Ed Peck. Dan O'Leary, possibly the most famous Indian fighter up until 1868, had guided a survey party for General William Jackson Palmer when he was looking for a railroad route through Northern Arizona in 1867. O'Leary and Ed Peck were always in the news during the decade of the 60s, because of their continued success in fighting Indians.

Eventually Sieber became foreman of a large ranch near Prescott. Here he was called upon to fight Indians on a regular basis. With the help of Dan O'Leary, he became most proficient in learning the rudiments of scouting. Sieber developed the keen ability to hear, see and smell, and accumulate and evaluate evidence. Upon this basis, he could make fast decisions about what was happening, what might happen and why it was happening at all. From his friend O'Leary, Sieber learned and learned well.

When Gen. Crook arrived in Arizona with orders to crush Yavapai and Apache resistance, Al Sieber was one of the first Crook sought to train and oversee his companies of Indian Scouts. Crook immediately admired Sieber's worth, and could see that he was a knowledgeable Scout.

General Crook needed men like Sieber, whose skills he described as extraordinary. Crook placed equal value on his other Scout leaders like Dan O'Leary, Archie McIntosh and Tom Horn.

Crook's plan to subdue the hostiles entailed placing small commands into the field to saturate the territory and either fight or keep Indians so stirred up that they would choose to surrender rather than starve or be routed out and slaughtered. Winter snows aided in this operation.

Crook's ruthless plans involved destroying the Indian's food supply and not only subjecting them to starvation, but also to freezing. In the later part of the Indian Wars, this became the general procedure of the army who used the winter months as their ally to hunt down, capture or kill Indians during their most vulnerable time.

Throughout the winter, soldiers and Scouts attacked, burned and destroyed encampments, wiped out food supplies and killed off the Indians' half-starved pony herds. After the Superstition Mountains were cleared of hostiles, the war moved east and west of the Verde River. By the first week of April 1873, bands of Indians began to surrender, most of them at Fort Verde. They complained that "every rock had turned into a soldier and that soldiers sprang from the ground."

The only one who did not surrender at first was Delchay, also known as "Big Rump." This Yavapai leader was considered the scourge of the Verde Valley by the soldiers and settlers alike. Every bit as elusive and treacherous as Geronimo or Billy the Kid, Delchay was often feared even by his own people.

In spite of the surrendering of these hostiles, this was not the end of the Indian troubles in Northern Arizona. Nevertheless, most of the white Scouts were discharged at the end of April, 1873. Archibald McIntosh and Al Sieber were not among those discharged, but were retained to mop up the remaining renegades.

Sieber was assigned to Fort Verde. From 1873 to 1879. He was the only regular guide and Chief of Scouts at Fort Verde during that time, and was continually in the field. Because the Indians at the Rio Verde Reservation, 16 miles from Fort Verde, were of mixed tribes, old feuds erupted regularly among these 2,000 people. It was common for many of them to bolt the reservation and have to be brought back. Sieber was convinced that regardless of the trouble at the Rio Verde Reservation, it was usually the old renegade Delchay who was at the bottom of it.

Delshay was as mean-tempered and sadistic as Geronimo. He was a powerful man, incapable of compassion, who cleverly was able to avoid capture. General Crook finally put a price on his head - literally. Payment would be received if Delshay's head was brought to him. Delshay's distinguishing feature was an ear ring which he wore in his right ear.

Three Tonto Scouts were sent out for the proposed capture or decapitation. Returning from their escapade, they claimed they killed Delshay at Turret Mountain on the 29th of July. They brought in a scalp with part of the notorious ear ringed ear as proof. Crook paid them for the scalp. On at least two different other occasions, Delshay's head was presented again to Crook, ear ring and all. Crook paid off all three parties. It wasn't until the final surrender of the Verde Valley Indians at Camp Verde on April 27, 1873, that Crook came face to face with Delshay, head in tact, when Delshay surrendered.

Six months previously, Delshay had 125 followers. Now only 20 existed. Delshay complained, "there was a time when we could escape the white-eyes, but now the very rocks have become soft. We could not put our feet anywhere. We could not sleep, for if a coyote or fox barks, or stone moves, we are up - the soldiers have come."

Delshay was finally killed by his own people on July 7, 1874. They were tired of being punished for his murderous behavior. His death was a real relief to Sieber. It finally gave him some spare time, to poke around for the yellow metal.

It is likely Sieber's Indian friends showed him the ancient mines near Fort Verde on what later became known as Jerome's Cleopatra Hill. Unfortunately for Sieber, he never filed an official claim on

Geronimo, 1870s. [FVSP]

the hill that later became the "Billion Dollar Copper Camp of Jerome." But in those days, copper had no particular value, the famous hill's gold and silver was buried too deep for him to know about, and the turquoise nuggets lying around were prized only to the Indians.

In 1875, Sieber was ordered to accompany 1,500 Indians from the Rio Verde Reservation on their infamous forced "March of Tears" to the San Carlos Reservation. After the Apaches and Yavapais were settled on this reservation, they entered into a new relationship with the white man. For many of them, their roaming days were over, and they wanted to live in peace. They were encouraged to forget their old ways and start raising corn instead of scalps.

After arriving at San Carlos, Sieber was assigned to be in charge of the first Apache police force, established by Indian Agent, John Clum. When Geronimo first bolted San Carlos in 1877, Sieber, Clum and 40 Apache policemen captured him and brought him back. When Geronimo escaped again in 1882, Sieber was once more put on his trail. This time, Geronimo's escape was precipitated by the Cibicue Mutiny of 1881. This was one of the only times when Indian Scouts mutinied against the U.S. Army.

CIBICUE MUTINY - AUGUST 30, 1881

In the majority of cases, a crooked Indian Agent could foment such trouble as to provoke an uprising on an Indian reservation. Such was the case of Indian Agent J.C. Tiffany at Fort Apache, who cheated in the issuing of rations, stole cattle meant for the Indians, and held back stores of supplies, selling them to unscrupulous others and pocketing the money.

The Office of Indian Affairs in Washington finally relieved him of his position, but it was too late. The harm had already been done.

A year before, a Piute medicine man named Wavoka had a vision in the Northern Plains of Nevada (Pyramid Lake) and the Ghost Dance was introduced. Shortly afterwards, the Indians at San Carlos adopted it.

Nockay-del-klinne, a White Mountain Apache, came forth with his own version of this new religion. His doctrine promised the resurrection of all ancestral Indians, dead warriors and relatives, and the restoration of land stolen from Indian people. Nockay-del-klinne envisioned the death and removal of all white men from their sacred homeland by the time the corn grew tall.

Ten years earlier, Nockay-del-klinne had been sent on a peace mission to Washington, and conferred with President Grant. Although only in his twenties, this young Apache was a man of some influence and considered a man of peace. Upon his return, he enlisted as an Apache scout, and was one of the first such scouts used by General Crook to track down hostile Indians.

In 1881, just before being relieved of his Indian agency control

- the corrupt Agent Tiffany informed Col. Eugene A. Carr, commander of troops at Fort Apache, that Nockay-del-klinne was to be arrested, or better yet be killed if he showed any signs of resistance. This Ghost Dance had to be stopped.

Col. Carr left Fort Apache with 23 White Mountain Indian Scouts, ten civilians, and three troops comprised of 121 troopers. Their destination was Cibicue Creek where they were to arrest and bring back to Fort Apache this young prophet of the new religion. This religion was particularly alarming because, for the first time, traditionally hostile bands of Indians were dancing the Ghost Dance - together. The overriding fear among the soldiers was that this dance would incite another major uprising.

There are two versions of what happened next - The soldiers' version and the Indians' version. According to army reports, Nockay-del-klinne agreed to come peacefully after considerable arguing and pleading on the part of the soldiers. The Indian version states that a Captain Hentig forced his way into Nockay-del-klinne's wikiup and dragged the young medicine man out by his hair, enraging the assembled Indians. Nockay-del-klinne was then put under guard in a tent.

The troopers and their entourage then made camp around or near the Indian encampment. Sergeant Dead-Shot, a White Mountain Apache Scout, asked permission of his officer to move his Scouts closer to the Indian campsite, because of supposed ant hills in their designated area. Suddenly, after they had moved closer to the Indian camp, Sgt. Dead Shot let out a war-whoop. He and his fellow scouts started firing into the soldier's camp, much to the surprise and horror of the soldiers. Capt. Hentig, the one accused by the Indians of humiliating their medicine man, was the first to be shot - in the back - as were five other troopers. The guards near the horses and grazing mules were killed instantly, and the herd driven off by the Indians.

When the firing started, the Sergeant guarding Nokay-del-klinne did as he had been ordered by Gen. Carr. He promptly shot the medicine man in the head. Nokay-del-klinne did not die immediately, and tried to crawl from the tent. This time, the troop bugler, seeing him trying to escape, shot him again in the head. This shot was fatal. Other witnesses say that a seargant grabbed an ax and decapitated Nokay-del-klinne. The fighting continued until night fall, after which the troopers buried their dead, eight in number. The bodies of 18 Indians including Nokay-del-klinne, his wife and six of the betraying White Mountain Apache Scouts, were left lying on the ground.

The Cibicue Mutiny provoked a whole new uprising. Raids continued against settlers and soldiers alike. Eventually, arrests were made of some of the White Mountain Apache Scouts who were involved in the Cibicue Mutiny.

In March of 1882, three White Mountain Apache Scouts: Sgt.

Dead-Shot, Skippy, and Dandy Jim, were found guilty of treason. They were publicly hanged at Fort Grant. Out of grief, Sgt. Dead-Shot's wife, it is reported, hanged herself from a tree at San Carlos that same day. As far as the military command was concerned, Carr had not used good judgment in engaging White Mountain Scouts to help him arrest a White Mountain medicine man.

Just before they were hanged, the doomed Scouts placed a curse on the attending priest and commanding officer. Both died of natural causes a short time later.

THE DEMISE OF GERONIMO

Because of the Cibicue Mutiny and the subsequent uprising, General Crook was called back to Arizona. He left San Bernardino with a company of 30 civilian volunteers, around 200 Apache and Yavapai Scouts, serving under Lieut. Gatewood, and Chief of Scouts, Al Sieber. Crook had successfully negotiated with the governors of Sonora and Chihuahua, Mexico, to have permission to cross over one another's border without consequences when in hot pursuit of hostiles. This, he believed, would ensure the capture of these renegades, who up to this time, roamed freely back and forth from one nation to another to their sanctuary in Mexico's Sierra Madre Mountains.

This new arrangement did indeed bring about the surrender of the most hostile Apache outlaws: Chato, Nana, Loco and the most infamous of all - Geronimo.

But once again, a familiar scenario developed - the first night after Geronimo and the others had been returned to the San Carlos Reservation, Geronimo got drunk, and away he went. Nana, Chato and their followers left with him. As a result, Crook came under severe criticism from General Sheridan in Washington. Crook tendered his resignation. It was accepted.

General Nelson Miles was assigned to replace him. Upon taking command, and not having the faith that Crook had regarding Indian Scouts, Miles dismissed most of them and replaced them with 5,000 white troopers.

Now we have an assembly of 5,000 troops, being called upon to destroy Geronimo and his enormous force of 38 renegades. Without using the Indian Scout Service, it took Miles 15 months to accomplish this feat.

One of his first efforts was to set up 30 heliograph stations to flash Morse messages from mountain top to mountain top. This network of stations was set up from Fort Verde to Fort Huachuca. Over 800 messages were sent during one period of four months. When Geronimo saw these mirror flashes, he thought they were magic and avoided the mountains all together.

Shockingly, another of General Miles' first orders was to exile all Mimbres and Chiricahua Apaches, including faithful Scouts from those bands, to a Florida prison. Among them was Geronimo's

74

Capt. Adane Chaffee [FVSP]

Out in the field, this was the method used to carry wounded back to camp.
[FVSP]

own family.

Although General Miles took full credit for the final capture of Geronimo, in actuality it was Lieut. Gatewood and a company of reinstated Tonto Scouts from the Verde Valley led by two Tonto Apaches, Captain Smiley and Ed Joe. It is to them that the credit should have been given for finally locating Geronimo again in the Sierra Madres Mountains. Gatewood, with the help of two Chiricahua interpreters, convinced Geronimo to give himself up. As their reward, Miles shipped all these Scouts and interpreters off to a Florida prison along with Geronimo and his followers.

For the record, Geronimo was perhaps one of the most captured renegades in Arizona history. Among those who laid claim to his capture on various occasions were General Crook, John Clum, Lieut. Emmett Crawford, Lieut. Gatewood, and of course General Nelson Miles. History has never credited the real heroes in Geronimo's repeated captures - The Indian Scout Service of Arizona.

After serving two years at the Florida prison, Geronimo lived the remainder of his life in Fort Sill, Oklahoma. He often collected money by posing for photographs, autographing picture post cards of himself, and carving bows and arrows for children. He was quoted as saying, "I am no longer an Indian - I am a white man." He bragged that it took 5,000 soldiers 15 months to finally capture him and his 38 followers.

Geronimo died of pneumonia following a drunken stupor, after falling out of a wagon in a shallow pool of water, face down in the mud.

BATTLE OF BIG DRY WASH

The Battle of Big Dry Wash, took place almost a year after the Cibicue Mutiny, and was a direct result of it. Some of the White Mountain Scouts involved in that mutiny, joined a small contingent of Apaches led by a renegade named Nan-tio-tish. Their bloody escapade would come to a violent end in a remote canyon in the Verde Valley.

When the army command returned to Fort Apache two days after the famous mutiny, they found that word had spread about the death of the beloved medicine man, Nokay-del-klinne. Enraged Indians went on the war path again. Renegades by the hundreds fled the reservation and began a relentless series of raids against civilians and soldiers alike. Almost immediately, 11 troopers and seven civilians, mostly farmers and ranchers, were massacred within weeks of the incident.

For five years, the Verde Valley had enjoyed relative peace. Because Fort Verde was inactive, it was ordered to be abandoned in December of 1880. Most of the troopers were sent north to fight the Plains Indians. The Army officially closed Fort Verde in July 1881.

Fort Verde Today - Looking across the parade grounds toward the Commanding Officer's house (right) and the home of the Post Physician. photo by Alan Caillou.

Officers and their wives on a post porch at Fort Verde, 1880s. [SHM]

The more than 200 people who had settled in the Verde Valley, hated to see the troopers go, and even protested the decision. Three months after its abandonment, the events at Cibicue and San Carlos, caused the Fort to be re-garrisoned on October 26, 1881.

By July 6, 1882, a band of 54 Cibicue White Mountain Apaches, led by Nan-tio-tish and some renegades, including Indian Scout deserters involved in the Cibicue Mutiny, went on the war path. These hostiles raided the San Carlos Agency, killed the Indian police Chief and seven other Indian policemen, then stole supplies, horses, guns, ammunition and headed north.

Brevet Major General Orlando B. Wilcox - commander of the Department of Arizona ordered the activation of twelve troops of cavalry, and two companies of Indian Scouts. The following troops were immediately called to duty:

WHIPPLE BARRACKS: Colonel Mason, 3rd Cav., commanding, left Whipple Barracks with Troops K and H, 3rd Cavalry and Troop H, 3rd Cavalry. Lt. Morgan was attached to this column, but pushed on ahead of it to join Company E, Indian Scouts in time to be part of the battle. The column itself arrived too late to participate.

FORT THOMAS: Capt. Drew, 3rd. Cav. Troops A, C, G and L. This column did not arrive in time to participate in the Battle of Big Dry Wash due to trouble with their pack train.

FORT McDOWELL: Capt. A.R. Chaffee, 6th Cav., Troop I, and Company E, Indian Scouts were in route from Whipple Barracks to his home station at Fort McDowell, when he was advised by messenger from Whipple to wait for Maj. Mason at Rye Creek. He did so until the 14th when he pushed on in pursuit of Nan-tio-tish.

FORT APACHE: Maj. A.W. Evans, 3rd. Cav., left Fort Apache with Troop E, 3rd Cav. (Lts. Hardy and Johnson); D, 3rd Cav. (Capt. King and Lt. Johnson); Company I, 3rd Cav. (Lt. Converse); E, 6th Cav. (Capt. Kramer and Lt. Cruse); K, 6th Cav. (Capt. Abbott and Lt. Hodgson). Also Lt. Dodd, Scout Keogh, four Scouts and Company B accompanied the above named companies.

The hero, one of many, was Capt. Chaffee, 6th Cav. Troop I. He sent a messenger to Fort McDowell for Chief Scout Al Sieber and Company E, Indian Scouts to meet him at Rye Creek. They thus crossed Nan-tio-tish's trail on the Mogollon Rim. It was on the 16th of July that Maj. Evans came upon the trail of Chaffee, who was now only a half day's march away.

Evans sent a patrol forward to bring Chaffee into conference. Chaffee related that the hostiles were only a half-day's march ahead of him, and they had discovered the white horses ridden by his troopers.

Maj. Evans instructed Chaffee at daylight to pursue the enemy and that he would follow with his four troops in support. Evans advised him that Lt. Converse's white horse troop would be placed in front of his column to possibly mislead the Indians into thinking only Chaffee's single troop was chasing them.

Nan-tio-tish took the bait. He never realized he was being pursued by all these different columns. He thought his only threat was the forty white horse contingent that he planned to ambush - this was his fatal mistake. He delayed leaving his camp at "General Springs" until he could see the pursuing column of white horses advancing in the canyon below the Mogollon Rim.

When Chaffee reached General Spring Camp, he left a note for Maj. Evans to send Lt. Converse's troopers to reinforce him as soon as possible. About eight miles north of General Springs, where Nan-tio-tish planned his ambush, the trail descends 800 feet into the almost vertical canyon of Big Dry Wash. The Indians barricaded themselves behind rocks in order to guard the trail up from the wash. At this point, the canyon is a little over 700 yards in width. This planned ambush was discovered by Apache Scouts, and they warned Chaffee in time to avoid a disaster.

This engagement was to be fought on the high mesa of the Mogollon Rim, set in an area with no shrubbery or underbrush, but thick with large pine trees. The crossing point in this canyon was held by the hostiles, and their fire covered every foot of trail coming up or going down.

Chaffee dismounted his troops on the south rim of the canyon. At this very moment, Lt. Converse, with his all white horse troops, dismounted and began firing across the canyon. Nan-tio-tish, thinking this group numbering 40 was all that he faced, was surprised to learn that the troops numbered more than 80 with still more to come.

A few hours later, around 3 p.m., Maj. Evans arrived with four more troops, without the knowledge of the Indians. Chaffee reported to his senior officer and was amazed when Maj. Evans told him to continue his plan of attack, as he relinquished his higher rank in favor of "you found them - it's your battle - proceed as you planned." Maj. Evans dismounted his troops some three hundred yards from the canyon rim, unseen by the hostiles.

Chaffee immediately ordered Lts. Cruse and Kramer, Troop E, plus his own Troop I with Lt. West commanding, to proceed in an easterly direction. He ordered Al Sieber's Indian Scouts to go east about a mile and flank the enemy to the right. Lt. Converse kept up a steady fire across the canyon. Indian Scouts under Lt. Morgan, 3rd Cav. plus Lts. Hardy and Johnson of the 3rd. Cav., Capt. Abbott and Lt. Hobson, Troop K, 6th Cav. were sent westerly to cross the canyon and then were instructed to head east to outflank hostiles from the left, thereby preventing their escape. A small number of men were left to guard horses and protect the pack train in case the Indians filtered through the defenses. The troops commanded by Lt. Converse held the point, in case the hostiles tried to slip past the chasm.

During this engagement, a ricochetting bullet struck a lava rock sending a sliver into Converse's eye, wounding him and putting him out of action. He later retired from the army as a Colonel, wearing a black patch over his left eye from that day of battle.

Lt. Cruse and Al Sieber and their scouts were on the north rim of the Dry Creek Wash, scouting the east flank when they discovered the Indians' pony herd. At this same time, Lt. Abbott on the west flank opened fire. Confusion reigned as Indians didn't know which way to turn. They just wanted to get away, so they rushed for their ponies. The ambush had worked in favor of the soldiers. It was a trap that led to the Indians' death.

One of the mule packers with Al Sieber's Scouts reported, "right in the middle of the fight, one of the Scouts saw two of his brothers and his father with the hostiles. He threw down his gun and ran toward his kin. Al Sieber called out for him to stop, but he did not comply, so Sieber raised his rifle, fired, and shot his own Scout in the back of the head."

Against Al Sieber's advise, the young Lt. Cruse, with his seasoned Scouts, charged the Indian camp. A young Scotsman, Joseph McLernon, standing to the left rear of the lieutenant, was killed by a bullet meant for Cruse. Lt. Cruse fired and killed the hostile. Cruse was awarded the Medal of Honor for his charge upon the hostile camp. Two other officers, Lts. Morgon and West, also received this medal, as did 1st. Sgt. Taylor.

Thus ended a day of slaughter. A raging storm swept out of the west the next day and prevented a continuation of the carnage. An Indian Scout called it the heaviest rain storm and hail he had ever seen. According to Lt. West, it was so miserable and paralyzing that "Maj. Chaffee got so cold and wet he had to stop swearing."

Under the cover of darkness and the storm, the hostiles who were wounded and were able to escape did so, making their way across the reservation line some 20 miles away. Troopers who came from Camp Verde via Crook's Trail, arrived at daylight the following day, "much out of temper," because they missed the fight.

The following day - details were sent out looking for bodies and hunting the wounded. They counted 22 dead hostiles with seven wounded. It was presumed that many others lay dead, their bodies concealed in cracks and crevices of the rocky formations. It was learned that many Indians died later from wounds received in the battle.

Lt. Hodgson, head of a patrol that occupied an area where the hostiles had been, heard groans during the night. The next morning while investigating, the troopers were suddenly fired upon. Gun smoke arose from behind a large boulder, betraying the direction of the shots. The soldiers took cover and opened fire. The troopers continued firing for a few minutes, but getting no response, charged and discovered a young Indian woman, about 18 years old, lying prone on the ground. She shielded her six month-old baby while drawing her knife. She attacked the soldiers who finally overpowered her and took her gun and knife. Three bullets was all that was left, the empty cartridges scattered beside her.

The young woman's leg had been shattered by a bullet. A make-shift stretcher was made and she was transferred for two hours on a tedious decent down the canyon wall to the soldiers' camp. She must have suffered terribly, but never a groan was heard, nor did she cry out when an Army doctor later amputated her leg without anesthesia.

The Battle of Big Dry Wash was the final major battle between Apaches and Troops in Arizona. Nan-tio-tish was killed and the question arises, what would Cochise, Geronimo, Victorio have done under the same circumstances that faced this renegade warrior?

Of the soldiers who participated in this final battle, two officers, and seven enlisted men were killed or wounded. Co. "E" of the 6th Cav. took the heaviest causality toll.

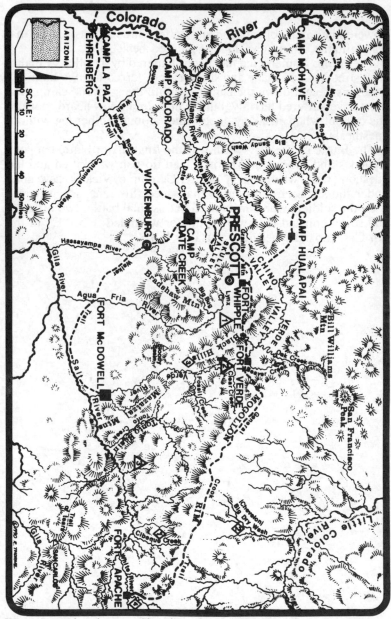

West Central Arizona - Showing places and names from this book.

⦿ Major Settlements   ■ Military Posts

△ Cattle Ranching: 1) King Woolsey, 2) William Wingfield, 3) Pleasant Valley.

◇ Indian/Military Skirmishs: 1) Cibeque, 2) Battle of Big Dry Wash,
3) Turret Peak, 4) Fort Apache

BIBLIOGRAPHIES

AL SIEBER, Chief of Scouts by Dan L. Thrapp, University of Oklahoma Press, 1964

NORTHEASTERN AND WESTERN YAVAPAI by E. W. Gifford, U. of California Publications in American Archaeology and Ethnology, 1936, Vol. 34

THE YAVAPAI OF FORT MCDOWELL, U.S. Department of Housing and Urban Development, Sigrid Khera, editor, Washington, D.C. 1978

JOURNAL OF AMERICAN FOLKLORE, Northeastern and Western Yavapai Myths by E.W. Gifford, Vol. 36, 1933

VERDE TO SAN CARLOS by William Corbusier, Dale Stuart King, Publisher 1968

RED MAN'S AMERICA by Ruth M. Underhill, U. of Chicago Press, Chicago and London, 1953, 1971

CARLOS MONTEZUMA AND THE CHANGING WORLD OF THE AMERICAN INDIANS by Peter Iverson, U. of New Mexico Press, Albuquerque, 1982

HISTORICAL ATLAS OF ARIZONA by H.P. Walker and Don Bufkin, U. of Oklahoma Press, Norman and London, 1979, 1986

YAVAPAI INDIAN HISTORIC CALENDAR, Yavapai-Prescott Indian Tribe, Prescott, Arizona 1990

1877: ARIZONA AS IT WAS by Hiram C. Hodge, The Rio Grande Press 1877, 1965

ARIZONA REPUBLIC, "Massacre Of 'Apaches' Recalled By Yavapais" by James E. Cook, Tuesday, December 29, 1987

ARIZONA REPUBLIC, History From The Other Side, "White Historians Say Apaches Died In Skeleton Cave, But Yavapais Heard It Differently." by James E. Cook, 1970

THE PHOTOHISTORIC PERIOD IN THE NORTH AMERICAN SOUTHWEST, A D 1450 - 1700, A review of Yavapai Archaeology by Peter J. Pillis, Jr., Arizona State University, Anthropological Research Papers No. 24, 1981

THE SOCIAL ORGANIZATION OF THE WESTERN APACHE by Grenville Goodwin, U. of Arizona Press, Tucson, Arizona

PIONEER STORIES OF THE VERDE VALLEY, As told by themselves and compiled by the book committee, The Verde Valley pioneer's Association, 1954

YAVAPAI PRESCOTT INDIAN TRIBE, brochure, Yavapai-Prescott Indian Tribe, 1989

VIOLA JIMULLA: INDIAN CHIEFTESS by Franklin Barnett, Yavapai-Prescott Tribe, Prescott, AZ. 1965

ARIZONA HIGHWAYS, "The Man Who Captured Geronimo" The Story of John P. Clum by Bernard L. Fontana, September 1990

ARIZONA: A CAVALCADE OF HISTORY, Marshall Trimble, Treasure Chest Publications, Tucson Arizona 1989

THE PEOPLE OF THE VERDE VALLEY, Plateau Magazine, Vol. 53, No. 1, Museum of Northern Arizona

THE SMOKE SIGNAL, Fort Whipple in the Days of the Empire by Andrew Wallace, Published by the Tucson Corral of the Westerners, Fall 1972

THE SMOKE SIGNAL, Camp Date Creek, Arizona Territory, Infantry Outpost in the Yavapai Wars 1867 -1873 by Sidney B. Brinckerhoff, Fall 1964, 1978

KING S WOOLSEY by John S. Goff, Black Mountain Press, Cave Creek, AZ. 1981

ON THE BORDER WITH CROOK by John G. Bourke, U. of Nebraska Press, Lincoln and London 1891, 1976

FORTY MILES A DAY ON BEANS AND HAY by Don Rickey, Jr. U. of Oklahoma Press 1963, 1972

DEATH IN THE DESERT by Paul Wellman, U. of Nebraska Press, Lincoln and London 1935

FORT VERDE STATE PARK LIBRARY AND MUSEUM

INTERVIEWS

David Sine - Yavapai-Apache, Camp Verde, AZ, 1989 - 90

Mabel Dogka, Yavapai-Apache, Kachina Point Nursing Home - Village of Oak Creek, Sedona, AZ. 1990

Louis Hood, Bernie Boyd, Sniffen Dickens, Fort McDowell Indian Reservation, Fountain Hills, AZ. 1990

The Elders of the Tribe, Yavapai-Apache Reservation, Clarkdale, AZ. 1989, 1990

Nancy Quaid, Yavapai-Prescott Tribe, Prescott, AZ. 1990

Vincent Randall, Tonto Apache historian and educator, Clarkdale, AZ. 1990

E
Eaton, Lt. George, 40, 43, 44
Echa-waw-cha-comma, 30
Ehrenberg, 27
Espejo, 11

F
Farfan, 11
First Territorial Legislature, 30
Fleury, Henry W., 29
Free, Mickey, 62, 63, 66
Ft. Apache, 72, 73
Ft. Lincoln, 27
Ft. McDowell, 22, 29, 33, 34
Ft. Verde, 27, 76, 77
Ft. Whipple, 28, 30, 52, 59, 60
Ft. Yuma, 25

G
Gaan, 20, 35
Gatewood, Lt., 74, 76
Ghost Dance, 72, 73
Gold Rush, 21, 24
Gregg, Gen., 31
Grief Hill, 31

H
Hakataya, 12
Halleck, Maj. General H.W., 30
Havasupai, 12, 14, 17
Hazzard, Dan, 69
Hohokam, 28
Hopi, 17, 18, 20, 21
Horn, Tom, 62, 67, 80

I
Incest, 1, 16
Ives, Lt. Joseph, 25

J
Jimulla, Viola, 52, 53
Jimulla, Walter, 52
Jordan, Walter, 50

K
Kakakas, 8, 20, 34
Kent Decree, 54
Kwevkapaya, 9, 12, 54

L
LaPaz, 27, 30, 31

Leihy, G.W., 29, 30
Legend of When Things Began, 1
Leroux, Antoine, 25
Loring, Frederick, 32

M
Maricopa, 14, 16, 17
Mingus Mountain, 2
Miles, Gen. Nelson, 74, 76
Mojave, 14, 21, 29
Moss, Capt. John, 29
Montezuma, Carlos, 54, 55
Montezuma Castle, 20, 56
Montezuma Well, 1, 3, 14, 20, 56

N
Nachez, 49
Navajo, 17, 18, 20, 21
Nantiotish, 76, 78, 79
Nockay-del-klinne, 72, 73, 76

O
O-hat-che-come-e, 32, 34
O'Leary, Dan, 32, 62, 69
Onate, 11
Ord, Gen. O.C., 31
Orm, Dan, 54

P
Pima, 16
Pinal Apaches, 28
"Pinole Massacre", 28
Poston, Chas., 28

Q
Qua-shac-a-ma, 28

R
Rio Verde Reservation, 36, 40, 48

S
Safford, Gov. P.K. 27
San Carlos Reservation, 37, 38, 47, 48, 49, 50, 72, 74, 78
Schuyler, Lt. Walter, 38 39
Seiber, Al, 40, 46, 62, 67, 68, 70, 72, 74, 78, 80
Sheppard, Molly, 32
Sine, DAvid, 7, 37, 47, 56
Sitgreaves, Lorenzo, 25
"Skeleton Cave Massacre," 34, 35
Skull Valley, 30, 47
Smiley, Capt., 50

Order Other Thorne Enterprises Publications For Your Enjoyment

THORNE ENTERPRISES PUBLICATIONS, INC. was launched in July 1988 with the successful EXPERIENCE SEDONA RECREATIONAL MAP. This map is now in its eighth printing with over 150,000 copies sold. It is the *only* map of the Sedona/Oak Creek Canyon area drawn to scale and was recommended by THE LOS ANGELES TIMES (1990); OFF-ROAD MAGAZINE (May 1991); and the NATIONAL GEOGRAPHIC TRAVELER (January 1992). Updated and completely revised in 1993, the new version contains a Sedona art gallery guide, a geographical column, and information on our area's new state parks, plus additional hiking, mountain bike, equestrian and off-road trails.

Retail $4.95 plus P & H

"With the help of a map called EXPERIENCE SEDONA, we explored red rock trails, the Mogollon Rim and vortex areas such as Boynton Canyon, touted for having psychic energy of the levels attributed to Stonehenge and the Pyramids of Egypt. I keep this map in the pocket of my car, next to my map of Italy."

Judith Morgan
The Los Angeles Times

Experience Sedona Legends and Legacies - This pioneer history of Sedona by writer/editor *Kate Ruland-Thorne* was first published in 1990 (5,000 copies) and is now its fourth printing. Among its many credits and rave reviews, was a recommendation by Elmer Dills on his show in Los Angeles during their eyewitness news feature on Sedona in 1990. 114 pages - 100 illustrations - historic site map.

Retail $8.95 plus S&H

"It's amazing that it took this many years for somebody to finally write the history of Sedona. After reading Legends and Legacies, it makes you glad nobody else tried." **Simone Butler** *The TAB*

"More delightful than her accurate, specific information, is her choice of topics and her method of presenting them.
Lois Stalvey, *The Sedona Red Rock News*

"Sedona's fascinating history comes alive in legends and legacies...an absorbing read." **The Sedona Red Rock News**

White Eyes, Long Knives & Renegade Indians *by V. Keith Thorne* - The Military history of General Crook's campaign against the Yavapai and Apache people of Central Arizona. 45 Pages, 20 Historic Photos, Map. **Retail $5.95**

"A well researched and fascinating account of General Cook's campaign in Central Arizona." **Col. Richard Norma** *U.S. Army, Retired*

Experience Jerome *by Nancy Smith & Jeanette Rhoda* -
"Jeanette Rhoda puts the reader into the underground tunnels and vast pits of Jerome's famed copper mines and in the offices of those who built fortunes on the treasures of Cleopatra Hill. Nancy Smith's excellent research is a must for visitors to Jerome who want to understand the boom and bust foundations of this world-famous hamlet."
Bill Roberts, *Editor / Publisher, The Jerome Traveler*

"Experience Jerome is a professionally written book that tells how a fascinating area got to be fascinating." **James Cook,** *Arizona Republic*

"The book is wonderful and I'm proud to be a part of it. I didn't realize Jerome and the Verde Valley was such a remarkable cleft in the world's crust. I'm very impressed and delighted to be aboard."
Rosemary De Camp, *Actress born in Jerome*

The Legacy of Sedona Schnebly
by Kate Ruland-Thorne
"I am grateful for the careful research and creative talent that led to Kate Ruland-Thorne's vivid and accurate portrayal of my great grandmother, Sedona Schnebly. Renderings such as hers keep alive the spirit of the woman."
Lisa Schnebly Heidinger   **Retail $5.95**

Adventures in Arizona
by Kate Ruland-Thorne
The only cartoon version of Arizona's history with timelines and work pages. Used by school districts throughout Arizona.   **Retail $6.95**

Thorne publications are available at numerous locations throughout Sedona and the state of Arizona. Distributed by Canyonlands and Treasure Chest.

Screw The Golden Years
I'd rather live in the past -
by V. Keith Thorne
A humorous look at growing old.   **Retail $6.95**

Screw The Golden Years - Book 2
Oh the joys of getting old
by V. Keith Thorne
A sequel, which is even funnier than the first!   **Retail $6.95**

For more information or to place an order call or write:

Sedona Books & Music
140 Coffee Pot Drive, Suite E-103-A
Sedona, AZ 86336
(928) 203-0711